D0856196

years of experience both in the corporate world and in running a fast-growing leadership development consultancy, Mackin has seen it all. She masterfully presents her position and then offers groundbreaking advice and practical strategies that, if followed by CEOs, senior executive teams, and heads of leadership development and talent management, will truly revolutionize this critical, nonnegotiable element of every business that absolutely will determine its success. I strongly recommend Leaders Deserve Better *for every CEO and executive in the world. Read it, internalize it, embrace it, and practice it, and you will see your people and your business flourish—as they should!*

—John Mattone

Author, The Intelligent Leader

Top executive coach

Leadership is how we achieve an outsized influence on events and others. Good leadership is the reason. No matter what the untoward circumstances or injuries to their shortstop, some teams always finish near the top. Jennifer Mackin understands those principles. Even more importantly, Jennifer can teach you and your team.

—Dave Oliver

Author, Lead On, Against the Tide: Rickover's Leadership Principles and the Rise of the Nuclear Navy, *and* A Navy Admiral's Bronze Rules: Managing Risk and Leadership

Rear Admiral, US Navy, Retired

Former CEO

LEADERS DESERVE BETTER

JENNIFER MACKIN

LEADERS DESERVE

BETTER

A LEADERSHIP DEVELOPMENT *REVOLUTION*

ForbesBooks

Published by ForbesBooks, Charleston, South Carolina.
Member of Advantage Media Group.

ForbesBooks is a registered trademark, and the ForbesBooks colophon is a trademark of Forbes Media, LLC.

Printed in the United States of America.

10 9 8 7 6 5 4 3 2 1

ISBN: 978-1-95086-326-6
LCCN: 2020908514

Book design by Megan Elger

This publication is designed to provide accurate and authoritative information in regard to the subject matter covered. It is sold with the understanding that the publisher is not engaged in rendering legal, accounting, or other professional services. If legal advice or other expert assistance is required, the services of a competent professional person should be sought.

Advantage Media Group is proud to be a part of the Tree Neutral® program. Tree Neutral offsets the number of trees consumed in the production and printing of this book by taking proactive steps such as planting trees in direct proportion to the number of trees used to print books. To learn more about Tree Neutral, please visit **www.treeneutral.com**.

Since 1917, the Forbes mission has remained constant. Global Champions of Entrepreneurial Capitalism. ForbesBooks exists to further that aim by bringing the Stories, Passion, and Knowledge of top thought leaders to the forefront. ForbesBooks brings you The Best in Business. To be considered for publication, please visit **www.forbesbooks.com**.

To my family: My husband, Carroll; my boys, Ethan, Lake, and Henry; and my mom, DeeAnna, for the freedom to continue my learning journey and your encouragement all along the way.
I love and appreciate you all!

CONTENTS

I f you have anything to do with developing leaders, there is a good deal of research that says you have a problem. It isn't from lack of trying. Substantial amounts of money are being spent. Numerous courses are available. Many people are involved. The problem is not in the effort; it is in the method.

Based on her review of relevant research and twenty-five years of personal experience, Jennifer Mackin makes clear that current practices aren't working. For many companies they aren't working now and didn't work in the past. Some of the main reasons for this lack of results are spelled out in this book. They provide a sound basis for self-analysis. An urgent need right now is for everyone involved to critically evaluate the results they are getting from their leadership development efforts and make the commitment to do it in a more productive way.

A four-part solution is presented that most companies could adopt. A real-life example makes the recommended solution easy to understand. The development of leadership capabilities for first-line managers and the second layer—managers of managers—is particularly important.

A better way to conduct management development, as described in this book, requires enhanced management involvement. Connecting the development activities to the strategy, providing face-to-face development activities, enabling on-the-job practice, and ultimately leading the effort are key contributions needed from management. How this plays out is the heart of this book.

—Stephen J. Drotter

ACKNOWLEDGMENTS

To all of my business partners:

Tom Cox, for having the confidence in the book's success and giving me the ability to work "heads down" for many months while taking care of business!

Kent Jonasen, for giving me clarity on what leaders are missing in their development and a new platform to support large initiatives.

Scott Kiefer, for being a confidant while building our two businesses for most of our careers and your flexibility to create new solutions to get the outcomes we always knew were possible.

I'd like to thank my ForbesBooks team for my entrée into my first book. Without their organization, support, and energy, this wouldn't have been written. Specifically, I turned to Summer Flynn and Caroline Nuttall, my idea people.

Lastly, I appreciate my dog, O'Reilly, for listening to me as I talk out loud—often.

J ennifer Mackin is a change agent at heart and a passion-
ate believer that the path of development is an ongoing and
lifelong journey. As a leader in two consulting firms—CEO
of Oliver Group, Inc. and president and partner of Leadership
Pipeline Institute US—Jennifer enables companies to *transform* by
inviting their leaders to revolutionize the way they develop people.
She has a bold goal for all CEOs and other leaders to connect people
victories with business victories. As an author and speaker with over
twenty-five years of consulting experience, she is a recognized leadership development influencer.

As one of the few female leaders in her industry, she heads a
growing national leadership consulting firm, and—through Oliver
Group and Leadership Pipeline Institute—has experienced teams of
consultants advising businesses all around the globe. Over the last
two decades, she has shared her message that *leaders deserve better*
with CEOs, human resources managers, leadership development
leaders, entrepreneurs, and other senior leaders in healthcare, hospitality, distribution, government, manufacturing, higher education,
banking, financial services, and social services.

Jennifer earned her BS in marketing from Indiana University in

Bloomington and her MBA from Owen School of Management at Vanderbilt University. She and her husband have three sons and live in Louisville, Kentucky.

'm ready to sound a warning, and it's a big one. In fact, if you're a CEO or are on your company's human resources team, please consider this book one giant cautionary tale. For too long, an alarm has been sounding in the corporate world, but no one has noticed—or everyone has pretended not to notice—because deactivating it requires time, effort, and a revolutionary new mindset.

I'm not alerting you about something imminently life threatening, like a tornado or a wildfire. But it is dangerous nonetheless. Why? Because having ill-prepared leaders is a crisis with ripple effects, and the long-term consequences of ignoring it are devastating. It's a company-wide—if not an economy-wide—issue that threatens the livelihood of everyone in the business world. The problem causes emotional and psychological hazards to caring, hardworking individuals—the ones who want to contribute their talents to the world, enjoy their jobs, and be proud of what they do—which is *everyone*, including your sons and daughters, neighbors, employees, and friends. It also affects *you as a leader*. Ultimately, business success is all about people success. You can't have one without the other. Without strong, happy, productive people in the workforce, the health of our teams, businesses, and communities is at stake.

Maybe this sounds a bit dramatic, but as president and CEO of Oliver Group and president and partner of Leadership Pipeline Institute (LPI) US, I have spent the last twenty-five years consulting with thousands of leaders and entrepreneurs in healthcare, hospitality, distribution, government, manufacturing, higher education, banking, financial services, and social services. During that time, I have observed industry trends, ownership transfers, and succession plans. What have I learned from my varied experience? That no matter the organization or industry, there is a crisis looming, and despite the efforts of our current leadership development, leaders aren't prepared, and development is failing.

Many CEOs complain that their people aren't ready to lead into the future. I think that's the *outcome* of the problem; the *source* of the problem is that leaders don't know what to do differently to strengthen their people. The leadership development world needs to wake up. This is a bigger problem than many realize. Without stopping by your corporate office or knowing your exact situation, I can tell you that your current leadership development practices are likely ineffective. I admit there is a lot of skilled delivery available, but despite quality content, it's landing flat. Leaders are not adopting what they learn, and that's a problem. In order to create transformational change, the information not only needs to stick in leaders' minds, but it also must be connected to the business strategy to fundamentally shift mindsets and behaviors.

When your leadership strategies aren't working, you're wasting resources—people and money. Despite companies spending close to $356 billion globally on leadership development in one year alone, they are not getting returns on their investments.[1] You can't afford to waste time and money using standard practices just because they're trendy or the way you've always done them. You can't look away from the failures of the present-day leadership development model. If you do, you lose.

CEOs and leader developers, here it is, my own customized warning—and it's directed at you: *if you don't make a revolutionary change in how you foster leaders, your businesses—and your people—will suffer.* In order to help your organization, you must transfigure it from the inside. This requires a new way of thinking about learning and development. It requires a leadership development revolution, and you can be the one to lead the way.

Through the following pages, I will share strategies for effective leadership development that is deserving of leaders so that CEOs and heads of HR can lead the revolution. To that end, this book will aim higher and teach you how to

- foundationally shift your mindset of how you think about leadership development,

- disrupt the broken development systems,

- amplify the potential of people, and

- transform the DNA of your organization by drawing a direct line from people victories to business victories.

The skills required of an effective leader haven't changed much in modern times, so what has created this dire situation? Look around. Because of the ever-evolving business world, you have to learn faster, decide sooner, and move quicker. As our culture gains speed, you

---

1   Michael Beer, Magnus Finnström, and Derek Schrader, "Why Leadership Training Fails—And What to Do About It," *Harvard Business Review*, October 2016, https://hbr.org/2016/10/why-leadership-training-fails-and-what-to-do-about-it.

won't have time to remedy this problem if you wait too long. You must revolutionize your development now. Things are moving that fast. And if you don't act soon, your business might not be prepared for what's coming.

Even as I was preparing the final draft of this book, the world became more volatile and chaotic than ever with the spread of the coronavirus. Most organizations had little—if any—time to prepare. Once businesses had to send their people home and shut their doors, there was no time for development. It was too late. This is exactly why we need to start the revolution today. Even when money is tight and the future is uncertain, we must think about doubling down on the development of leaders and people. Preparing leaders for chaos and disruptions is exactly what traditional development is lacking. In a health and economic crisis such as this, companies will suffer even more without effective leaders.

Prepared leaders are more adept during unforeseen disruptions and are able to pull their teams together, even without the luxury of proximity. They can recraft a new, realistic strategic direction quickly, communicate how each employee fits into the new direction, and help their people work efficiently to increase the viability of their companies. Leaders must remain calm and steady to handle challenging decisions like layoffs, project postponements, investment slowdowns, and more. During times of crisis, such as a global pandemic, leadership means helping people feel safe, showing them an immediate path for the near term, and maintaining a sense of direction. Communication can't be erratic or inauthentic but instead must acknowledge the problems, share accurate information, and provide hope. It sounds like a profound responsibility because it is.

CEOs, heads of HR, and senior leaders, it's time to revolutionize your people development. In order to change your teams' behaviors, you must first change your mindset. You need to be honest with yourself about your responsibility to your business or organization. The reality is that you will never check the leadership box off for good. If you check it off, you're doing it wrong.

I know that a lot of you will have reasons why you haven't enriched your leadership development strategies already: you're worn out; you don't have the time, money, or people to enact change; you think what you're doing is working, but you aren't measuring successes. These are all valid excuses, but quite frankly, they are irrelevant. Let's establish now that there will always be barriers; there will always be a myriad of obligations vying for a leader's time. With this book, I want to show you a way around these obstacles so that you can maximize your time, efforts, money, and people.

In Part I of this book, we will delve into why current development is ineffective. We will look closer at standard leadership delivery methods to determine why they didn't work in the past and don't work in the present. In Part II, we will focus on solutions to these problems and explore how integrating the Four Drivers of Leader Development Success can revolutionize your organization and your teams. Furthermore, I have created a tool, the Leader Development Maturity Tool, that can help you understand how the development practices you have adopted are leading you to the overall goal of leader readiness based on several factors.

THE FOUR DRIVERS OF LEADER DEVELOPMENT SUCCESS:

1. The overarching people strategy must be connected to the business strategy.

2. Leadership development must be leader-led.

3. Leaders must be able to put into play the skills they learn.

4. Leadership development must have face-to-face components.

I'm not here to simply point out the problems, though there are enough to fill these pages; I'm here to offer you—and beg you to implement—a solution because leaders deserve better. Step one: stop developing how you've always been developing. Step two: keep reading to discover strategies that offer transformational change. You can start developing your leaders differently today to prepare them for tomorrow. Let's get the revolution started.

PART 1

WHAT'S THE
PROBLEM?

CHAPTER 1

Think Your Standard Leadership Development Is Working? Think Again

've lost count of the number of eyerolls I've seen when mentioning an upcoming leadership program. Just the thought of attending a development session seems to exasperate many people: *I don't have time to leave my job for training. They're never helpful, and I just get behind in my real work.* I can't fault them for their reactions; in fact, I admit that much of traditional leadership development is tedious and ineffective.

Despite how wearisome some programs are, those in roles to develop leaders hold pivotal roles in the sustainability and viability of corporations and organizations around the globe. It is our job to provide tools and skills to "functional leaders," "leaders of leaders," and "leaders of others." In my experience, 99 percent of leaders seek to learn and grow stronger and more effective in their work. Understandably, those leaders cannot enhance their ability alone because it is impossible to know what is required at each stage of their careers. New learning, however, enables them to excel and flourish. Leader developers, it is our responsibility to provide what is needed to encourage growth for every person—and every role—within our organizations.

Despite the honorable reasons many of us are drawn to the field, however, our good intentions are not enough to fix what's broken. Though we may not feel directly responsible for human civilization, we are charged with doing our jobs well. It's not a valid excuse to say we are doing what all other organizational developers are doing. Though it may be true, and not our fault, it is our responsibility to do better because our leaders deserve better, and there are better approaches.

In *The Succession Pipeline*, authors Stephen Drotter and John Prescott place the responsibility of people development on leaders, not Human Resources: "While employees retain much responsibility for their own development, managers inherit the obligation to train and develop their people with their first appointment as supervisor. The responsibility grows with every assignment."[2] Whether or not senior leaders think they have the resources for people development, it is an inherent responsibility that demands their attention.

We can't stop developing leaders. Though markets and industries may change, the reliance on leaders will not.

Though the standard leadership development isn't working, it is still essential. We can't stop developing leaders. Though markets and industries may change, the reliance on leaders

---

2   Stephen Drotter and John Prescott, *The Succession Pipeline: How to Get the Talent You Need When You Need It* (Carlsbad: Motivational Press, 2018), 182.

will not. Traditionally, most leaders were groomed in-house. In the 1970s, for example, only 8 percent of S&P 500 CEOs were recruited from outside the company.[3] By 2015, the rate of outsider appointments rose to 14.3 percent, and by 2017, that number surged to 44.4 percent.[4] These numbers are directly correlated to the failures of standard leadership development. If companies are effectively grooming in-house leaders, then they don't need to go elsewhere to find talent. Recruiting from outside the company is a costly and time-consuming endeavor, and if boards of directors, advisers, and CEOs are often resorting to this measure, it means a lot of people aren't doing their jobs.

The recent rise in executive search firms further suggests there is in fact a "war for talent," specifically a "war for leaders." I recall one of my clients who needed a key role filled from the outside, and she paid 1.5 times the market compensation to draw talent away from their current roles. In addition, they paid 32 percent of the first year's compensation for the recruiter to identify this talent. As the authors of *The Leadership Pipeline* assert, "These overly aggressive, sometimes desperate attempts to recruit outsiders suggest that the leadership pipeline is inadequate. Internal training, mentoring, and other developmental programs aren't keeping the pipeline full, making it necessary to look outside."[5]

So what's the answer? First, as leaders, we need to take responsibility for the growth and development of our people. Next, we ought

---

3   Jason D. Schloetzer, Matteo Tonello, and Melissa Aguilar, "CEO Succession Practices: 2015 Edition," *The Conference Board*, April 2015, https://www.conferenceboard.org/publications/publicationdetail.cfm?publicationid=2935.

4   Jason D. Schloetzer, Matteo Tonello, and Gary Larkin, "CEO Succession Practices: 2018 Edition," *The Conference Board*, October 2018, https://www.conference-board.org/publications/publicationdetail.cfm?publicationid=8093.

5   Ram Charan, Stephen Drotter, and James Noel, *The Leadership Pipeline: How to Build the Leadership-Powered Company* (San Francisco: Jossey-Bass, 2001), 1.

to rethink the standard leadership development practices. We should develop our leaders in-house using programs that excite them and inspire them. We need to build leaders today that we can rely on tomorrow, and we need to accomplish this with fewer eye rolls and more high fives.

THE EVOLUTION OF LEADERSHIP DEVELOPMENT

Before we get further into the problems leaders are facing, let's take a moment to look closer at the evolution of leadership development. I'm often asked if company leaders are born as leaders or developed into leaders. The answer is *both*. The term "leadership" has been in the lexicon since the 1700s and was used to describe certain people— specifically those who imbued the traits of a leader. Behaviorists called this "trait theory," and it presumed that leaders were born, not made. It wasn't until the seminal Ohio State Leadership Studies of the 1940s that this theory was debunked. Researchers concluded there were no discernable set of *traits* that explained effective leadership; instead they claimed that certain *behaviors* were associated with leadership.

Once these behaviors were identified, the military and corporations began considering how they might capitalize on the dissemination of leadership through training and development. It wasn't until the 1980s, however, that a study showed that these initial leadership training programs did not facilitate organizational change. In fact, a more recent four-year study that followed six large corporations found that company-wide leadership programs merely created "the fallacy of programmatic change."[6] Though we have known for some

---

6   Russell Eisenstat, Bert Spector, and Michael Beer, "Why Change Programs Don't Produce Change," *Harvard Business Review*, November–December 1990, https://hbr. org/1990/11/why-change-programs-dont-produce-change.

time that these programs do not affect outcomes, we have continued delivering the same stale messages through the same tired approaches.

For decades since this "fallacy" was uncovered, companies have soldiered on anyway, proceeding with the same leadership "trainings" just to check the box, perform their due diligence to develop their teams, and move on. After all, some training is better than none, right? According to data from the 2018 *Chief Learning Officer* Business Intelligence Board, despite the research that our standard development programs aren't working, 94 percent of organizations either planned to increase or maintain their level of leadership development spending in 2019.[7] In addition, large US organizations (with more than one thousand employees) increased their leadership staffs by 12 percent.[8]

So why are we still spending time and money growing our people development only to do the same thing we've always done, despite the research that it doesn't effect change? It's irrational, wasteful, and shortsighted, but before we jump into the solution, let's take a closer look at the problems—and the corresponding consequences for companies and organizations if they don't address them.

WHY DEVELOPMENT FAILS

Since I've been in the industry over the last twenty-five years, the skills of a leader have only slightly changed. They have always needed to be able to coach and connect with each individual, set direction and follow up, hire the next high performer, and more. In more

---

7   Mike Prokopeak, "Follow the Leader(Ship) Spending," *Chief Learning Officer*, March 21, 2018, https://www.chieflearningofficer.com/2018/03/21/follow-the-leadership-spending/.

8   Dor Meinert, "Leadership Development Spending Is Up," *Society for Human Resource Management* (July 22, 2014), https://www.shrm.org/hr-today/news/hr-magazine/pages/0814-execbrief.aspx.

recent years, leaders are now also expected to cope with chaos, manage increased information flow, and improve communication across a group of employees as diverse as ever. All of these skills are not only helpful—they are essential.

There are many reasons why leaders fail, and some are specific to companies and industries, but most often one leader fails for the same reason all leaders before her did: inadequate development. Our leaders deserve better! It's time to be frank about the ways we are disappointing our leaders and our businesses. If you are a senior leader and don't like criticism, then take a deep breath, and steady yourself for the honesty that lies ahead.

> It's time to be frank about the ways we are disappointing our leaders and our businesses. If you are a senior leader and don't like criticism, then take a deep breath, and steady yourself for the honesty that lies ahead.

1. Leaders Aren't Trained for Leadership

There are massive oversights in how we develop leaders. Firstly, we wait too long to train them. Research that looked at *Harvard Business Review*'s database of over seventeen thousand trainees found that most of these leaders operated within the company for over a decade, on average, before receiving training on how to lead.[9] A decade! It is alarming to consider how many untrained managers are currently leading teams all over the world.

Can you imagine if a surgeon performed her duties for a decade before receiving training? Or if a contractor built houses for years before actually learning the skills of his trade? It's absurd to consider,

---

9   Jack Zenger, "We Wait Too Long to Train Our Leaders," *Harvard Business Review*, December 17, 2012, https://hbr.org/2012/12/why-do-we-wait-so-long-to-trai.

yet it's standard practice when it comes to people development. Much of this disconnect is because of the intangible nature of leadership jobs. Many jobs are skill based. Mechanics know how to fix cars; dentists know how to fix teeth. But leaders? What *exactly* do they do? There are certainly skills involved, but the ambiguous nature of the role is perhaps part of the challenge.

One major problem is that leaders don't always think they need to be developed. When leaders don't have what they need, an easy remedy would be to ask for help, but therein lies the challenge: asking for help. Too often, leaders believe they are expected to know how to do their jobs and have a hard time asking for help because it makes them vulnerable and thereby puts their position at risk.

The reality is that leaders don't know what they're missing. They don't know what they're going to need because they've never done other higher-level leadership roles before. It's time to rethink the stereotypical, invulnerable leader. There is no place for this staunch superiority in leadership. No one actually expects a leader to be indomitable; in fact, some of the most effective leaders are honest about their limitations and seek to address them.

2. Leaders Maintain the Same Workload and Expectations

There's another reason leadership development fails: potential up-and-comers return from specific development to the same workload and expectations they had prior. Even if the program covered relevant material, without a concrete plan to incorporate the new skills into leaders' daily responsibilities, the learning won't stick.

Unconnected knowledge that is not applied to workload and expectations is rarely integrated. Countless times, I've witnessed high-quality development fail because an organization's infrastructure doesn't support leaders changing where they spend their time and the type of work they do. Rewards, performance measures, and accountability all play vital roles in establishing expectations and ensuring that development is assimilated.

3. Leaders Don't Possess Leadership Mindsets

In order to be a leader at any level within a function, you've got to have a leadership mindset. We will talk more about this throughout the book, but for now, it's important to establish that a leader's main job is to develop people. I know this sounds basic. It is! Yet it is one of the greatest challenges in the field because leaders don't know that is their number one job.

If you are a leader, you are responsible for the people who report to you and for their development. That is your primary job. This requires you to shift your mindset away from the area you work in. For example, a promoted accountant might now lead people but still spends 90 percent of his job doing accounting tasks. Instead, over time, 10 percent of his time should be spent on tasks and 90 percent on preparing others for the tasks.

Leaders must ask themselves, *What value do I create for the company in my role as a leader?* Creating value is no easy undertaking and requires leaders to spend their time differently and development dollars to be spent differently. There is no other option. This is the only way forward.

4. Organizational Development Professionals Lack What They Need

Many leader developers are unsupported by CEOs. Part of the reason for the disconnect between delivery and implementation is because CEOs are not driving the overall development plan. Many CEOs I have worked with admit they didn't realize it was their job to design and help execute people strategies. When they don't take responsibility, there isn't an intentional focus.

There needs to be a partnership between CEOs and HR in order to get the best outcome from the leadership teams. As authors Drotter and Prescott assert, "HR cannot be just another voice at the table. They must be the expert voice … "[10] When the leadership development department is unsupported, all of the money and time being spent on training is wasted, and CEOs eventually find themselves without people ready for the next business phase or a succession plan for the future.

Senior leaders don't always value leadership, which is an unfortunate reality. Because of this, they often don't invest in it or connect it to their productivity and success. Many companies allot too little money, or no money at all, to their people development. Or if they do spend resources on it, they don't tie it to strategies or individual development plans, so the information exists in a vacuum and isn't integrated.

The most common objection I hear is that companies don't want to spend their resources on development, and they don't want to devote employees' time to their development. When I get an objection around money or time, I realize I haven't successfully connected people development with business success in their minds. Instead of fighting the money or time battles, I focus on solutions and how our work with them will produce capable leaders for the future. I ask, "What will the outcome be if you choose not to do something different? What are your other choices for solving this problem? Do you see lost productivity? Turnover?" When I can connect intangible development with such tangible results, I can start to shift the mindsets of senior leaders and ensure allocation of resources toward development.

Oliver Group and Leadership Pipeline Institute ask individuals

---

10   Stephen Drotter and John Prescott, *The Succession Pipeline: How to Get the Talent You Need When You Need It* (Carlsbad: Motivational Press, 2018), 35.

to spend on average four consecutive days with facilitators to understand the fundamentals of leadership at their level. After that, we ask them to devote a few hours each month continuing to reinforce and build on that foundation. That's not a lot of time, especially when you consider that these are the areas that will propel the business forward and ensure its enduring success.

Many companies don't find the development of leaders significant until they are readying for succession planning, embarking on a new venture, or weathering storms that threaten their viability. This reactive approach is risky because development takes time. Conversely, a proactive strategy for development prepares people/leaders for inevitable chaos and change.

5. Organizational Development Professionals Are Rarely Strategic Thinkers

Leadership development executives are typically trained in organizational development, human resources, and/or psychology. They learn how to design organization charts, build and deliver content, and oversee leadership programs. Oftentimes, however, the leader developers have never led others outside of a few people in their departments. They are teaching people to lead without having been leaders themselves. See the issue? If trainers and facilitators haven't led at the level they're teaching, they cannot be nearly as effective.

Traditionally, the people who are drawn to leadership development enjoy teaching and watching people grow. They aspire to help individuals gain knowledge and be successful. Sounds noble, right? So what's the problem? Leadership development executives are trained professionals, but in my experience, many aren't strategic thinkers, so they're not likely to connect the dots between the strategic goals of the organization and what they need to do to get leaders ready to meet those goals.

Senior leaders might tell organizational development professionals what they feel leaders need to be successful. They mention that their leaders need to be strategic, navigate change, or communicate better, so then the leader developers put programs together around those topics, but they're not connected to the overarching strategic direction because organizational development professionals aren't privy to the direction. They then focus on specific competencies in a vacuum. When development plans are disconnected from the strategy, they are doomed to fail, which sets leaders up for failure as well.

6. Organizational Development Professionals Don't Measure Success of Development

Even when a leader does get development, it's rarely measured. For example, a company might want to promote an individual who requires more leadership training, so they send them to a university. The employee attends the classes and learns the content, but then what? Most return to their jobs not understanding how to execute what they learned. Many organizations don't gauge leaders' effectiveness in leading other people, so instead they're being appraised using metrics of revenue, quality, and service. Because the company doesn't understand how to assess leaders, the leader herself doesn't know either; again, a leader doesn't know what she doesn't know.

This is one of the most common problems I see: few organizations go as far as measuring success by knowledge transfer and behavior change that is specifically tied to the program content. If you can't measure these metrics, then you don't know what works and what doesn't. Development is useless if leaders aren't held accountable to

Development is useless if leaders aren't held accountable to put the information in play.

put the information in play.

THE VALUE OF EFFECTIVE LEADERSHIP

We are at a crossroads where the need for leadership development is recognized but the implementation itself isn't working. Companies might understand logically that having strong leadership in place fortifies them, even though they might not fully understand how or why.

With strong leadership, the payoffs are massive. According to Deloitte, provider of global research in HR, "The companies that rank top in leadership development maturity invest 30–40% more money in leadership than their peers."[11] Furthermore, if you consider Aon Hewitt's study of the Top 25 Global Top Companies for Leaders, you find they spend almost 35 percent more per manager on development than others.[12]

These numbers show that leadership development is a force multiplier of success and creates more retention across the board, including decreased hiring costs and better overall performance. From working closely with CEOs, I have found some common impacts of effective development.

11   Josh Bersin, "It's Not The CEO, It's The Leadership Strategy That Matters," *Forbes,* July 30, 2012. https://www.forbes.com/sites/joshbersin/2012/07/30/its-not-the-ceo-its-the-leadership-strategy-that-matters/#2cc65ace6db8.

12   PRNewswire, "Aon Hewitt, The RBL Group and Fortune Announce the Global Top Companies for Leaders," *Aon,* November 3, 2011, https://aon.mediaroom.com/news-releases?item=78793.

FUNCTIONAL IMPACT OF LEADERSHIP DEVELOPMENT:

- Clear line of sight for all employees between business strategy and objectives cascaded throughout organization, denoted by enhanced strategic thinking

- Effective span of influence for work groups or functions enhanced through greater ability to inspire through effective communication

- Alignment of responsibility and accountability

- Achieving versus doing culture

- Commitment versus compliance culture

- Succession readiness for key roles

POTENTIAL FINANCIAL IMPACT OF LEADERSHIP DEVELOPMENT:

- Higher employee engagement

- Lower employee turnover

- Higher customer satisfaction

- Stronger financial performance

- Speed of succession in key roles

Leaders are responsible for the people who implement and execute the company's mission each day. When you consider the life cycle of an employee, you start to understand the value in leadership. A new employee, for example, typically doesn't initially know how to perform her job. Naturally, her function and performance within the company changes as she develops new skills. A leader's job is to direct that employee's evolution for the betterment of the company's mission and purpose. There aren't many aspects of a business more important than this. I've watched many clients start new employees without needed guidance, support, direction, and motivation from the leader. As the leader, if you're not developing your people, providing the knowledge and resources they need to do their jobs, then you aren't doing your job.

Right out of college, I had the choice between three career opportunities: selling insurance, joining the sales/marketing department of Glidden Paint, now PPG, or working in American Trans Air's (ATA's) rotational training program. I chose ATA for three reasons—the flying perks, the ability to help out my grandmother who lived in Indianapolis, where they were headquartered, and the management trainee program. For a year I rotated between departments—travel agency, finance, route planning, and marketing. After that year, the manager sat me down and asked where I wanted to work. With full conviction, I declared, "Marketing."

As expected, I began my career at the lowest level of marketing. I didn't have a job description; they just started giving me work to do. I had never been more bored in all my life. My duties included choosing music and food for the planes, editing flyers, and calling travel agents to get them to use our airline more often. One afternoon after I had finished all my work, I wondered, *What should I do now?* I reached out to my boss to let her know I had completed *X*, *Y*, and *Z* projects. "What else can I help with?" I asked hopefully. She looked up from her work and said, "Nothing. I can't think of anything. Thanks for asking." Deflated, I turned around and went back to my desk with nothing on my task list. That is when I started looking for another job.

If someone—especially in marketing—had taken an interest in my development or sought ways that I could add skills to the team, I wouldn't have become disengaged, and I wouldn't have left. If somebody at ATA had even said, "I need you to stick in marketing for a couple of years, and then there will be a potential next step for you," I probably would have stayed because I would have felt like I was working toward something meaningful. This small shift would have made a huge difference in my level of engagement and my loyalty to the company.

This didn't necessarily lead me on the path to leadership development, but it did motivate me to look into recruiting, because I understood the power of picking the right people for the right roles. This is how I ultimately landed at Oliver Group. My personal experience is a good reminder of how leadership development continues to fail people. Too often we develop leaders from the top because it pays off more quickly. When we overlook the value of new employees, however, we are blocking their paths to future leadership. This is one reason standard leadership development fails: it focuses on the present leaders without much regard for future leaders.

Research shows that the lowest per-person share of leadership development funding—$2,600 per person—is given to first-level leaders, which is 34 percent less than emerging leaders and half the amount of midlevel leaders.[13] Despite not receiving the same investment, these first-level leaders manage an average of nine to eleven direct reports while adjusting to their new leadership roles.[14] And they're doing so with little to no development! As leaders, we have to do a better job for those who work for us. We have opportuni-

---

13   Dor Meinert, "Leadership Development Spending Is Up," *Society for Human Resource Management* (July 22, 2014), https://www.shrm.org/hr-today/news/hr-magazine/pages/0814-execbrief.aspx.

14   Ibid.

ties to be intentional with our direct reports, and we must use those opportunities to engage them today to prepare them for leadership tomorrow.

Leaders are responsible for building and fostering the culture of the workplace. Businesses focus on their mission and core values but not as much on how to drive execution and performance. Oftentimes we get so fixated on—or perhaps overburdened by—products, services, and metrics that we forget there are human qualities like engagement, fulfillment, and actualization to consider. When employees can tap into these qualities, companies benefit, as discovered by a 2018 Gallup survey:[15]

> Organizations and teams with higher employee engagement and lower active disengagement perform at higher levels. For example, organizations that are the best in engaging their employees achieve earnings-per-share growth that is more than four times that of their competitors. Compared with business units in the bottom quartile, those in the top quartile of engagement realize substantially better customer engagement, higher productivity, better retention, fewer accidents, and 21 percent higher profitability.

If we don't know how to live, breathe, and disseminate our business values, then we aren't actually creating a culture.

Culture is tied to engagement, which is tied to results. As I learned in my early years at ATA, people have to be engaged in order to accomplish high-quality work. But who is responsible for

---

15   Jim Harter, "Employee Engagement on the Rise in the U.S.," *Gallup*, August 26, 2018, https://news.gallup.com/poll/241649/employee-engagement-rise.aspx.

that engagement? You guessed it: the leaders. If we don't know how to live, breathe, and disseminate our business values, then we aren't actually creating a culture. We're merely designing a poster for the wall. If the people within the business can't identify with the mission and purpose, customers won't either.

The workforce in America currently employs more than one hundred million full-time workers.[16] According to Gallup data, one-third of those employees are engaged in their work, meaning they are satisfied, content, and find purpose in their jobs; conversely, 16 percent of employees are "actively disengaged" and are miserable in their work environments. Perhaps most disturbing of all are the remaining 51 percent, who are not actively engaged or disengaged, but are "just there."[17]

Why does engagement matter? Because it's directly linked to employee satisfaction and business outcomes. According to the same Gallup data, the engaged workers outperformed the disengaged ones in real, measurable ways.

---

16   Gallup, "State of the American Workplace," 2017.

17   Ibid.

ENGAGEMENT'S EFFECT ON KEY BUSINESS OUTCOMES

When Gallup analyzed the differences in performance between engaged and actively disengaged business/work units, work units scoring in the top half on employee engagement significantly outperformed those in the bottom half on nine crucial performance outcomes.

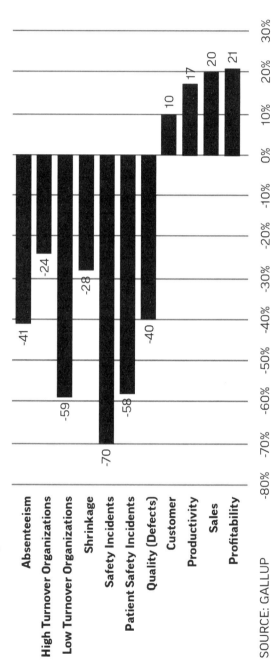

Outcome	Value
Absenteeism	-41
High Turnover Organizations	-24
Low Turnover Organizations	-59
Shrinkage	-28
Safety Incidents	-70
Patient Safety Incidents	-58
Quality (Defects)	-40
Customer	10
Productivity	17
Sales	20
Profitability	21

SOURCE: GALLUP

Leader developers are rarely trained to consider their teams' engagement, yet much of the satisfaction or dissatisfaction—70 percent, according to the data—is related to the manager.[18] Nevertheless, The Predictive Index's 2020 State of Talent Optimization report found that, among six hundred executives across twenty industries, only 55 percent regularly "diagnose their employee engagement data" of those executives, and only 22 percent took the time to identify what was driving the disengagement.[19] We can see from these statistics that senior leaders are not taking engagement seriously. In fact, only 17 percent of executives rate it as a top priority. Nevertheless, engagement matters, and it's up to the leaders and leader developers to address it.

According to Jim Clifton, Gallup's chairman and CEO, engagement studies "indicate an American leadership philosophy that simply doesn't work anymore. One also wonders if the country's declining productivity numbers point to a need for major workplace disruption."[20] I think Clifton is being kind. There is no doubt that the leaders and the leader developers are failing, and it's time for the "disruption" that Clifton alludes to.

Development leaders must understand that their role is not just to facilitate training; they are the bridges between the people who work there and the meaning they seek. It's human nature to enjoy work when you feel your potential is maximized and you are being

---

18   Ken Royal, "What Engaged Employees Do Differently," *Gallup Workplace*, September 14, 2019, https://www.gallup.com/workplace/266822/engaged-employees-differently.aspx?utm_source=workplace-newsletter&utm_medium=email&utm_campaign=WorkplaceNewsletter_November_TEST-A_110519&utm_content=learnthepatternsofbehavior-TextLink-1&elqTrackId=97b6e749911746afacd443b665445891&elq=6d06ab293ef246cdbaa0d6c75d902bd6&elqaid=2545&elqat=1&elqCampaignId=587.

19   The Predictive Index, "The State of Talent Optimization Report," 2020, 54, 55.

20   Gallup, "State of the American Workplace," 2017, 3.

challenged. People want to feel like they have a purpose, and they want to—need to—understand how they contribute to the whole.

Development leaders must understand that their role is not just to facilitate training; they are the bridges between the people who work there and the meaning they seek.

When an employee who answers phones, for example, sees how his individual role connects with a broader mission, he's excited to be there. It's the leaders who must make it real for the employees, and there is no greater mission than this.

People don't quit a job, the saying goes—they quit a boss. Or in this case, a leader. Of course, leaders can't be fully responsible for the engagement and satisfaction of each employee, but without time and effort spent building the environments and pathways to success, your team will be weak, and your efforts will be stymied.

You must invest in leadership for the resiliency of your company or organization. CEOs spend a lot of time on other areas—like business acquisitions and board negotiations—but if you don't have your people ready for progress, then you are wasting your time. Your efforts will fail without robust teams to bolster them. Without strong leaders, you will not be able to compete. That's the ultimate bottom line.

CHAPTER 2

Current Development Doesn't Cut It

Since 1984, Oliver Group has always been focused on the readiness of people and putting the right people in the right positions. Our vision was clear from the beginning, and we have remained committed to it, despite how our company has evolved. We started as a provider of The Predictive Index assessments, primarily to CEOs. We believed that if leaders had objective data about people, it could help them in all realms: Who is the best candidate for each position? What is the best way to communicate with them? What are their needs? And how does the company fill those needs? We understood that capturing and delivering this information could lead to greater employee performance and satisfaction.

Over time, we began to realize that assessments that are not tied to a larger context aren't as helpful as they potentially could be. We were in a vacuum, and we were not solving all of the problems we wanted to. For example, our assessments identified gaps in the organization's teams and in its leaders, but we had to take that a step further to fill those gaps with the right people receiving the right development. From there, we started to design and deliver courses to develop specific competencies for the groups that had "gaps" in their knowledge. This is how our leadership development practice began in 1986.

We started to focus more on leadership development—not just with CEOs but with human resources (HR) as well. Soon, we were partnering more with HR to get their teams what they needed. It was always our belief that in order to effectively use the assessments, the data had to be understood by the CEO, in particular, and the senior team. HR had to be a partner in this to help drive it through the organization, but without the senior team's involvement and understanding of its value, the process was ineffective. It was more apparent to us that the head of companies weren't as involved in development as they were in other decisions.

Over time, as we learned more, our delivery changed; in addition to offering up to a week of training, we were offering once-a-month programs for a year's duration. This allowed us to work with the same group of people—usually first-line leaders—on overarching topics so they could essentially become effective leaders in one year. Were our methods successful? Did our evolutions over time affect outcomes? I didn't know for sure. We were doing the best with what was available, but was it enough?

TRADITIONAL METHODS OF LEARNING

Many organizational development professionals do what everyone else is doing because that's just how it's done. As I began to see during my early years at Oliver Group, adhering unquestionably to the status quo is rarely the best pathway to success, especially since there are many problems with the traditional method of development. Now we ask clients a lot more questions up front to get a sense of their philosophies toward their people and their current processes, challenges, and successes with development. We ask what their expectations are for leaders beyond a job description. Typically, they can articulate what they want from their leaders for the next year or two. We link all of this information to ensure our programs and assessments are effective.

In the early 1990s, however, the process of providing organizational development went like this—HR would contact me to develop supervisors in a company. They would relay the areas that needed training, and we would go to work creating four days or more of content around communication, self-awareness, decision-making, and how to be more strategic, for example. We crafted a mostly lecture-based presentation that included minimal interaction. During the training, I talked, and they listened; it was understood that they would absorb it and then implement it. Leadership development for that company? Check. Done.

Where did I go wrong? Firstly, I didn't pull the CEO and HR leaders together to align them around leaders' needs. Oftentimes, CEOs have backgrounds in sales, finance, or operations, but rarely in HR. This sometimes means that HR doesn't have the same seat at the leadership table, and CEOs often don't know how to best leverage their HR team's expertise. Traditionally, many HR departments report to the general administration, finance, or operations departments, as seen in the sample organizational charts. This is a problem.

Ideally, we need to combine the CEO's strategic thinking with HR's ability to identify what people require. There needs to be partnership between the two for any leadership program to function properly. A poor organizational structure can stymie even the most effective leader development plan. The HR leader should report to the CEO, not the CFO, COO, or chief administration officer. Employees and development do not get the same visibility and weight without reporting to the CEO.

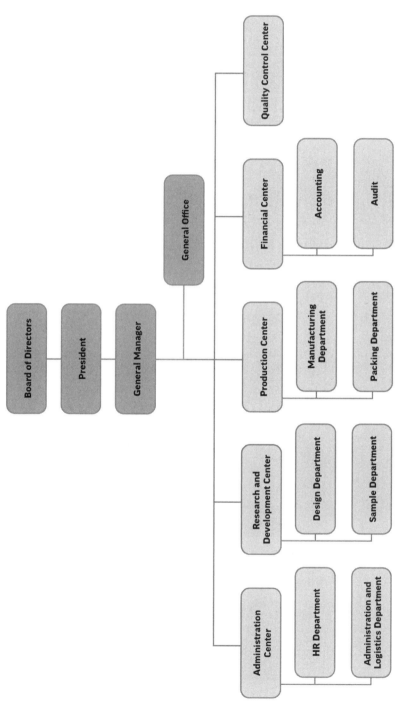

A poorly structured organizational chart that places HR under General Administration

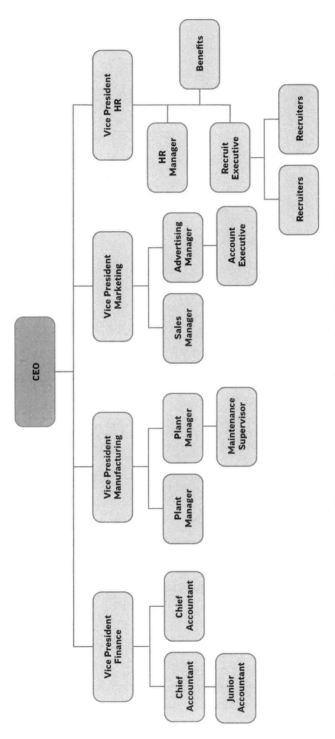

A well-structured organizational chart that places HR under CEO

The next blind spot I had in my early days of leader development was in my initial communications with the client. I asked about the areas the HR person thought needed to be developed, but I never questioned how he came to that conclusion or how it related to the company's larger mission. Since I didn't know, I couldn't provide that context to the cohorts. Therefore, they didn't know what their performance was being measured against, nor did they know what they needed to ask for in order to meet those expectations. This meant the leaders could not fill out an individual development plan because they do not know how to use what they learned.

The next mistake I made was offering training when I should have offered development. Most leaders cannot distinguish between training and development. Once you put them in a room, however, and they're facilitated rather than lectured to, they'll get the difference. Training—as it was then and is now—is topic-based information usually offered during onboarding or during periods of transition. It's typically done in a classroom or online setting and addresses specific topics a leader needs to know. It's the offering of information with the assumption that you will learn it and can access it when you need it. Training is concerned with the transfer of knowledge in a more limited, direct scope.

Development, on the other hand, deals with more intangible themes, like how to coach individuals. Its topics are more foundational and ongoing. These are ideas that need to be put into practice in various scenarios to be fully integrated. Like training, development involves the transfer of knowledge, but it also must be put into practice. Whereas you can "master" the information offered in trainings, development concepts are ongoing and never fully mastered. Like leadership itself, there is always more to learn and more to put into play.

The goals of development are readiness and being prepared for a variety of scenarios. If, for example, you transition from a start-up to a corporate environment, you can still use the leadership development tools—altered slightly—to be successful. When leaders are developed, they have a shift in mindset. Rather than being "taught to," they're coming to their own learning, their own conclusions, and their own planning.

In order to take full advantage of our leaders' potential, we must completely rethink the way we deliver development programs. This falls to the organizational development professionals. We must stop doing it the way we've always done it and embrace proven methods that are more efficient, successful, and dynamic.

WHAT KIND OF PROGRAMS DON'T WORK TO DEVELOP LEADERS?

- Academically taught programs
- One-off trainings
- Self-taught leadership
- Online training

Academically Taught Programs

Oftentimes, companies will send their leaders to outside universities to "fill the gaps" in their business training. The executive programs are taught by high-level, well-educated MBA professors who deliver concentrated development on the side. These professors often aren't practitioners. This means they are not in the workplace and certainly haven't led others, so the content is often more theoretical.

Let's be frank: universities don't change quickly, so the content is sometimes outdated or delivered through traditional methods that have been proven ineffective. For example, while taking my MBA classes, I didn't learn how to lead. I learned functional expertise such as finance, accounting, operations, economics, and marketing, but I never learned leadership. To this day, I don't know of many business school programs that offer leadership courses. If we send our leaders to academic institutions only, will they be more effective?

These programs can work if you're teaching specific skills, like how to read financial statements, for example; otherwise, the problem with these programs is that they don't help the cohorts put the practices into play. They don't know how it relates to their particular situation because there is no real context. The information exists in a vacuum, and unfortunately, there it stays.

One-Off Trainings

This is the program I described in my opening example. This was the standard transaction, early on, between myself and clients. They would tell me the specific skills they needed their team to learn. We'd create the content, deliver it, and then we were gone.

These programs are now used for topics like communication or bias in the workplace. Recently, some of our clients have requested diversity one-off training to increase the number of diverse leaders overall or give employees awareness about the need for diversity and inclusion. These are vital topics, but I've found that one-offs do not lead to retention or integration of the material. When organizations measure success, their numbers—the number of diverse leaders, for example—don't change. They have great intent, but they will not alter outcomes if they continue to rely on trainings that are proven to be ineffective.

Self-Taught Leadership

Some employees who participate in self-taught programs do so at the direction of their bosses. Perhaps they need to learn Excel spreadsheets, for example, so they're told to get the help they need. Other times, they might be struggling with something they don't want to bring to their bosses, so they seek out solutions through or online instruction. Though these can be effective for some situations and can augment the execution of their development plan, they are not the ideal ways to learn and integrate new material for the masses.

Digital Training

Online digital learning can be self-taught or as part of a company's online learning system. This is a growing tool since cohorts can access training anytime from anywhere. Though it has its obvious advantages, it has shown to be ineffective for leadership development. For reasons we will explore later, research on human learning shows that participants need to be engaged differently for leadership development. This is best done with human connection rather than online modules.

TRADITIONAL METHODS OF MEASUREMENT

Traditionally, it wasn't just the methods of delivery that failed future leaders; it was also the ineffective measurement tools. From the beginning of leadership development, it was understood that there needed to be some metric to gauge training effectiveness. This gave rise to the pervasive use of smile sheets. Smile sheets were feedback response forms to gauge cohorts' responses to training. They were called smile sheets because they measured how a participant "felt" about the experience using smiley, neutral, or frowny faces. If the facilitator got mostly smiley faces, it made her feel she had done her job well and could check off another training session, but it didn't measure whether the participants learned anything they could actually apply to their work environment afterward. For years, we allowed these simple smile sheets to give us an inflated sense of success and approval. As long as our smile sheets were positive, our clients were happy, and we would continue development.

Overall, how would you evaluate this course?

very poor				average					excellent
1	2	3	4	5	6	7	8	9	10

How applicable do you think this course will prove to be "on the job"?

not applicable				average				very applicable	
1	2	3	4	5	6	7	8	9	10

Please circle your evaluation of the following:

Level of difficulty	appropriate	too easy	too difficult
Amount of material	appropriate	too easy	too difficult
Pacing	appropriate	too easy	too difficult
Enough Practice	appropriate	too easy	too difficult

How would you rate the instructor's knowledge of this subject area?

very poor				average					excellent
1	2	3	4	5	6	7	8	9	10

How would you rate the instructor's presentation style?

very poor				average					excellent
1	2	3	4	5	6	7	8	9	10

Would you recommend this course?

not at all				moderately				very highly	
1	2	3	4	5	6	7	8	9	10

A sample smile sheet from Oliver Group's early years.

Since smile sheets were the standard feedback form, we didn't question it. Were the students better prepared for their jobs after training? We didn't know. Was revenue going up after sales leaders were developed? No idea. The general consensus was that smile sheets were better than nothing, so that's what we did. And we continued to do it that way for years.

What we didn't know at the time was that smile sheets didn't actually measure attendees' preparedness to put into practice what they had just learned. In fact, author and leadership consultant Will Thalheimer argues that "more than any other practice in our field, they [smile sheets] have done the most damage."[21] They not only failed to give appropriate measures of outcomes, but they also actually damaged the organization's potential. Leader developers understand that with valid learning measures, we can improve our content and maximize learning. This is not only our mission as organizational development professionals—it's our job.

In order to maximize measurements, we had to think about how people learn best. Smile sheets were typically given at the end of events. What we have learned from the science of human learning is that testing someone right after a concept is introduced only measures their understanding. We were not considering how much of the information they would actually apply and integrate. Thalheimer noted, "If we measure at the end of the learning event, the learners are at their highest level of memory retrieval … We are getting biased results. We are getting results that make us—and our learning interventions—look a whole lot better than the truth."[22] As you can see from the following diagram, smile sheets were only

---

21   Will Thalheimer, *Performance-Focused Smile Sheets: A Radical Rethinking of a Dangerous Art Form* (New York: Work-Learning Press, 2016), xx–xxi.

22   Will Thalheimer, *Performance-Focused Smile Sheets: A Radical Rethinking of a Dangerous Art Form* (New York: Work-Learning Press, 2016), 8–9.

capturing the initial learning curve without acknowledging the forgetting curve inherent to human learning.

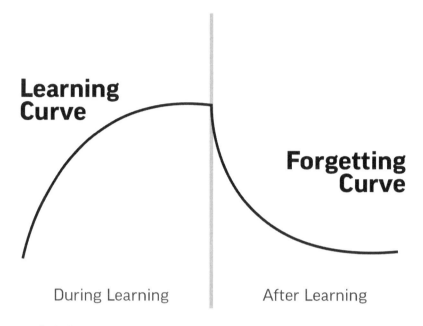

Will Thalheimer's "Learning and Forgetting Curves" are based on his research on human learning and forgetting.[23]

The Leadership Pipeline Institute strives for retention of knowledge and stickiness of the information in hopes of inverting the forgetting curve. On average, our client's leader survey results show 90 percent of knowledge retention right after the program and 85 percent retention six months later. With numbers like these, we know cohorts are retaining, not forgetting. Now that we have a broader understanding of human learning, organizational development professionals have to wake up and alter their methods of delivery and measurement. There is no excuse to continue to follow the status quo when it has been shown to damage the leaders and organizations we are tasked to support.

---

23   Ibid.

WHAT'S CHANGED?

There is no lack of leadership development programs, but the reality is that traditional programs are empty. They're disconnected from the business, so leaders are getting further behind, and we're not addressing it. Though I now recognize there are profound problems with standard leadership development, I admit that for years, I was part of the problem. I did what others did because that's just how it was done. I started to question many of our processes but had no framework for how to adapt to the outdated methods.

In 2010, Oliver Group, along with several other top consulting firms, was invited to hear Kent Jonasen, head of Leadership Pipeline Institute (LPI) Global, speak about new advancements in leadership development. His methodology was based on the book *The Leadership Pipeline*, by Ram Charan, Stephen Drotter, and James Noel. In the book, the authors offered a philosophy and a framework for developing leaders. As the head of HR for A. P. Moller-Maersk, it was Jonasen who decided to adapt those concepts into a curriculum that started the Leadership Pipeline Institute.

> *Though I now recognize there are profound problems with standard leadership development, I admit that for years, I was part of the problem. I did what others did because that's just how it was done.*

Like the book's authors, Jonasen was interested in how to ready a pipeline of leaders. He concluded that what clogs that pipeline is when leaders are not leading at the level they're supposed to—specifically, when they lead one level below them. For example, if you're a supervisor, you're often doing the individual contributor work; if you're a leader of leaders, you're often directly involved with individual contributors who report to leaders instead of leading at a higher level. This was an innovative way of thinking, and when I heard it for the first time, it clicked.

It made sense to create programs around this framework philosophy and design with quality measures on leadership skills, skill adoption, and behavior change. When Jonasen tested his ideas on three thousand leaders at Maersk, all metrics increased, including behavior change, knowledge retention, and improved service and quality metrics. This program worked better than anything he had ever done. When I attended the one-day overview of the program, I was astounded by the innovative thinking.

THE LEADERSHIP PIPELINE INSTITUTE PROGRAMS

- were connected to measures,

- based their methods on interactive delivery,

- encouraged a shift in mindset, and

- focused on work values, time application, and skills.

Everything they shared was connected to measures. Gone were the smile sheets of the past. Their surveys were thoughtful and based on human learning retention and research. Furthermore, their delivery was unlike any of the standard programs. LPI programs were interactive, with little lecturing. Programs were driven by participants sharing and learning from each other. Though this sounds like a subtle distinction, it showed a profound shift in mindset. Rather than hold a training mindset, it encouraged a facilitator mindset. Even from the one-day overview, it was clear that humans learned better through interactive, participant-focused programs. No one was rolling their eyes at being in the room. Instead, participants were lively and engaged. It was a dynamic example of how collaboration can drive innovation and engagement.

LPI also acknowledged that different levels of leaders need different skills. If you're an individual contributor doing a job, you're responsible for the work; if you then move up and are leading other people, you have to shift where you spend your time and what work you value. Most importantly, you have to value developing other people. Though this sounds logical, this is not often integrated into standard development programs.

LPI acknowledged that work values, time application, and skills needed to be developed in these individuals, so their programs valued that. Cohorts whose jobs had foundationally changed in this way could then be developed in these new areas—*What does leading others mean? What are you being measured on now that you weren't before? And how do you do that?* This understanding helped cohorts function in their new roles with greater understanding of how their work values, skills, and time application altered within their new role.

Once I better understood how the needs of leaders had changed, I could better meet those needs. I understood that many aspects of the industry remained unchanged. For example, communication and being strategic were still essential. The actual content remained similar. The need to review performance and offer feedback was still required. What had changed? The methods of learning and the measurements had evolved, a person's connectivity with her boss throughout the process of learning had changed, and the follow-up with the facilitator and the organization to ensure development was being leveraged had altered.

I recognized that Jonasen's approach was superior to the current development our clients were leveraging, and stronger than Oliver Group's offering, so I decided to shift with clients. It took us two years to fully transition to this new model and become an LPI partner to expand this thinking throughout the United States.

With our new understanding of the innovation in organizational impact, we had to rethink how to measure company impact and not just individual impact. We discerned that smile sheets are the lowest measure. We needed to know not only the information that was understood right after a learning event but what information was retained and integrated after learning. The next level of impact we needed to ascertain was whether a person learned new skills. And finally, the highest measure of impact was to determine whether a person's behavior changed. Using these concepts, Oliver Group quit using smile sheets, adopted the LPI's measures, and created an impact overview based on the Results Pyramid created by the authors of *Change the Culture, Change the Game.*

We adopted and adapted the model based on concepts that were designed to help a leader understand the likely stages that individuals and/or teams would need to go through to drive different results through true behavioral change. The baseline was that the leader had to engage people around their development, and that had to be coupled with knowledge. From there, as confidence was built and new behavioral practices tested and put into play, different results would occur.

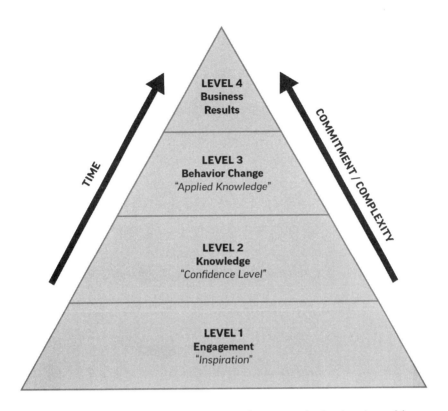

The Oliver Group's Impact Overview Pyramid serves as a leader thought model on individual and team change.

Oliver Group started to include the model in all proposals so that organizations would understand the importance of discussing, agreeing on, and tracking the progressive impact of their investment. It allowed us an outline for how we think about measuring impacts that may otherwise not be recognized or identified in the organization, and it helped to distinguish what we should be looking for in our cohorts over time.

Though the measure remains important, the context has become equally as important. I would no longer use the standard process to develop and design programs to meet an organization's needs without asking more questions: What's driving the need for this? How does it connect to your strategy? What have you done in the past? If this is successful, what does that look like? What levels are these individuals? An organization's *why* has become supremely important, and we can't move forward if we don't know what that is.

> An organization's why has become supremely important, and we can't move forward if we don't know what that is.

Since we look more at context, we can now design programs that are connected to bigger solutions. We look at the entire company to determine what everyone needs by level. Only then can we determine where we start. This allows us to have a wider company impact than just with one group of people.

WHAT'S AHEAD?

Oliver Group has been putting these development innovations into play for almost a decade. We have long-term measurable outcomes that show the effectiveness of our approach. We now measure leaders' skills before people work with us, right after, and then six months later. This allows us to look closer at knowledge retention, because if you don't retain the knowledge, what's the point of offering it? From the work we've done, we've assessed that on average, teams start with 45 percent knowledge before training. After training, we see that percentage increase to 90 percent; six months later, they retain 85 percent. Those numbers show great outcomes and are what all leadership developers should be striving for.

These measures let us know that not only were participants engaged—the lowest level of measure—but they also had knowledge retention. This creates inspired and confident teams. In addition, the numbers show that the knowledge was applied, which affected behavior. Together, these results enhanced company outcomes and business results.

As I was working on this chapter of the book, I spoke with a seasoned head of HR at a manufacturing company who uses our services fully. We were talking about how much the industry has changed, yet so few companies are adjusting. I asked him, "You've been in this industry a long time. Do you feel like your leaders need to morph?" He exclaimed, "Absolutely!" When I pressed him further about what aspects he thought were different, he wasn't sure.

This is a common blind spot: CEOs and HR professionals are aware of the company and industry changes but are unaware of how to prepare leaders for them. That's why the responsibility falls to organizational development professionals to stop using standard methods and measures that don't work. Leaders deserve better than one-off trainings and programs that won't make a difference in their abilities or in your organization's success. I've found a better way, and it works.

CHAPTER 3

Evolve or Face Extinction

t's a common misconception to think only flailing businesses have failing leadership development. The truth is that all businesses, no matter the size or industry, can be taken down by inept leaders—or more commonly—the absence of leadership. One of Oliver Group's clients is a large global retail business that boasts over 150 leadership development professionals. You would think that with this many people focused on developing leaders, they would have dozens of leaders in the pipeline readied for succession planning—a process for identifying and developing new leaders who can replace old leaders when they leave, retire, or pass away. The reality, however, is quite a different story.

If an organization has no pipeline of leaders ready to take over senior leadership positions, then a lack of succession planning can be catastrophic for even the most enduring company—as this global retail company learned. No matter the age and achievement of a business, it needs to continually work on its succession planning efforts. As our workforce's demographic continues to change, companies that have these plans will become a major factor in an organization's viability.

We were initially contacted by this company's chief marketing officer, who worried that though they had eight vice presidents (VPs), none of them were ready to take over as senior VPs (SVPs). As the chief marketing officer neared retirement, this void of prepared leaders was becoming more worrisome each day. As she looked to the future, she realized she wouldn't be able to retire, or the department would suffer if they didn't ready their younger leaders today for senior positions tomorrow. She knew her VPs didn't have the presence to be at the table with the other senior executives, but she didn't know what else they were missing.

Once Oliver Group was brought in, we knew we needed to better understand each individual's capability to determine if one or two needed one-on-one coaching to shore up an issue, like a behavioral challenge, for example, or if the entire group needed development in different or similar ways. I shared with her the typical competencies and behavioral changes that needed to happen to shift the VPs to the senior level. We focused on the five areas of Functional Leaders as determined by LPI.

FUNCTIONAL LEADERS CONTENT OVERVIEW

Be a full member of the business team	Drive functional excellence	Coach and hold direct reports accountable	Select leaders and build the function	Taking ownership of developing leadership talent
• Value what you do not know • Integrate with and appreciate other peer functions • Become full member of the business team	• How your function adds value to the business • Execute your functional strategy • Build meaningful KPIs • Build functional competitive advantages	• Develop a coaching leadership style • Set SMART development goals for leadership performance • Build accountability and credibility around your performance process	• Recruit direct reports based on their leadership potential • Build an agile and execution focused function • Lead through multiple layers • How to disclose leadership potential in interviews	• Identify leadership talent • Build the leadership pipeline • Develop leadership talent • Dynamic and strategic talent management

PERSONAL DEVELOPMENT PLAN AND EXECUTION PLAN

WORK VALUES AND TIME APPLICATION ADJUSTMENT

LEADERSHIP BEHAVIORS AND LEADERSHIP PERFORMANCE INDEX® SURVEY

Source: Leadership Pipeline Institute

Once she reviewed and understood these functions, she was able to discern that many VPs had some, but not all, of these abilities. Though all VPs had fairly equal potential to take her role, none of them were ready. We decided to develop them in all areas. In addition to this program development, the CMO also agreed to six months of group coaching to reinforce their learning and make sure these skills and behaviors transferred to their daily work.

After the program, we had monthly calls with the eight VPs to find out how the continued development was going and what barriers, if any, were in their way. As is sometimes the case in readying her leaders, we uncovered some larger systemic problems. How did we discover this? Because on every call, at least one VP would get emotional: "There's no way I can do my job. The SVP expects us to do our direct reports' work. I'm not able to work at the functional level I have learned about. This isn't going to change." It was clear; the leaders were overworked, overwhelmed, and uncertain things would ever change. They didn't see the path to be the leader they knew they needed to be after attending the program.

So what went wrong? We delivered programs that research has shown to be effective, which we could control. What we couldn't control was senior leadership's involvement. We based our methods on interactive delivery connected to measures, mindset shifts, work values, time application, and skills. Without senior leaders to address the larger systemic issues uncovered after our programs, the environment couldn't support the development we provided. This is the unfortunate reality of being a consultant and having limited control of outcomes. We can design the most dynamic programs available, but if senior leaders are not involved, there is a chasm that no development leader can cross.

This is another example of why development doesn't work without the involvement of senior leaders. It isn't enough to go in and deliver content—even strong content—with the expectation that it will make all the difference. Sure, you might transfer some competencies, but cohorts will undoubtedly return to their work, and then the reality hits that they still can't focus on developing people as their main responsibility. Without someone internal to 1) evaluate what's in the way of implementing new leadership foci, and 2) remove barriers for leaders, no program is going to work. In this retail business, the CMO could have supported these leaders differently by talking with them one-on-one about their daily work and helping them execute the development plan they created during their learning process.

Organizational developers must have conversations with leaders and senior HR people about how to measure success of programs and learning up front, which Oliver Group and LPI US does with all clients. If we have those conversations first, then we can foresee systemic problems like this company encountered and fix them to make the process easier on participants. Otherwise, we can deliver all the development in the world, but it won't address the larger issues that are burdening the developing leaders.

The reason this example is important is because, despite the size of this global business, their problem is a common and universal one. Like many others in the same positions, these VPs understood the company's development vision was important, but they couldn't spend time on it because they didn't have people under them ready to support them.

When readying leaders, one of the most common and detrimental problems is that leaders cannot delegate below, and they do not get support from above. It is a systemic failure, and it has the potential to bring down even the largest of organizations. If you're a senior VP, you have to spend time on development with your VPs. It's your job; it's your livelihood. Leadership becomes a house of cards, and without a supportive foundation, you cannot build higher, and eventually the whole house collapses.

When you have a high-level leader, they should be delegating a lot more—that's how you build your people—but this large global retailer couldn't. Furthermore, because the senior VP didn't have the time to spend—because she, too, couldn't delegate and was overworked and overburdened—there was no support on either side. As a result, within a six-month period, three out of eight VPs left.

Why did they leave? They had too much work because they were expected to lead their team and work a level down. They should have had a team of people to do all of these things they were stressed about. They left because they didn't see a way out. They knew the only option was to work harder for longer hours. They were already working hard, with little time for themselves and their families. Understandably they started questioning, *Is this all worth it?* For some, the answer was a resounding *no*.

This was not ideal for the individuals themselves or for the company, because those developed leaders took all of their development with them—at a critical time when the organization was focused on its succession planning. They were working at a high level for one of the biggest companies in the world, so where would they go from there? Most likely they would end up in a similar situation with no one under them to whom they could delegate. They might find another company, but they also perhaps encountered the same problems. If a company of this size—with so many people charged with readying leaders and so many dollars spent on that mission— couldn't do it, most businesses don't stand a chance.

This organizational failure creates a larger problem across industries as people shuffle from one organization to another, looking for someone who has a development structure in place that can allow them to flourish to their full potential. As a result, leaders today are never really getting what they need. They just shuffle from place to place, searching. Meanwhile, companies worry about the lack of leaders available. They talk about the "war for talent" as if there isn't anything they can do about it, when in reality it's a failure of organizational developers and senior leaders. The time to enact change is now. Our environment will continue to grow more volatile, and you have to ready your teams. If you wait, your organization will suffer.

OLD PROBLEMS, NEW GENERATION

The challenge of succession planning will soon hit all organizations, regardless of size or industry, as the demographics of the workforce continue to change and baby boomers reach retirement age. Baby boomers have maintained their hold on the labor workforce for years. Peaking at 78.8 million people in 1999, baby boomers have been the largest living adult population.[24] By 2016, however, there were an estimated 74.1 million boomers; by 2050, that population is expected to dwindle to 16.6 million.[25] These changes will directly affect many organizations' senior leadership positions. Ready or not, most organizations will soon be faced with succession planning.

Despite this impending demographic shift in the workforce, few companies are addressing the need for succession planning. Large companies in particular are weak in this area, with successors identified for only 10 percent of their first-level leaders, 19 percent of their midlevel leaders, 24 percent of senior-level positions, and 36 percent of executive

---

24 Richard Fry, "Millennials projected to overtake Baby Boomers as America's largest generation," *Pew Research Center*, March 1, 2018, https://www.pewresearch.org/fact-tank/2018/03/01/millennials-overtake-baby-boomers/.

25 Ibid.

positions.[26] These aren't great numbers considering they indicate how well prepared (or not) these organizations are for the future.

Authors of *The Succession Pipeline* assert that "the only sustainable solution to talent shortages is to grow your own."[27] Rather than wait for superstars to walk through your organization's doors, Drotter and Prescott encourage senior leaders to commit the entire organization to developing talent. This process starts with senior managers who must share "a clear philosophy of talent development."[28] Sound familiar? Once again, we are looking to senior leaders to lead organizations through the impeding workforce evolution.

Succession planning requires CEOs to be strategic thinkers. They have to think long-term and proactively. If they are shortsighted or reactive, the organization can't survive disruptions. First, CEOs need to identify which roles are key to the company's viability. Next, senior leaders must assess the potential and performance of emerging leaders who could potentially fill leadership positions. Finally, senior leaders must provide these key individuals with development by level to fill the gaps in their experience and understanding. As you can imagine, none of this happens quickly. This is why senior leaders must be involved in all development and strategy so that any systemic organizational issues can be addressed and mitigated. This is how an organization evolves and avoids extinction.

---

26 Dor Meinert, "Leadership Development Spending Is Up," *Society for Human Resource Management* (July 22, 2014), https://www.shrm.org/hr-today/news/hr-magazine/pages/0814-execbrief.aspx.

27 Stephen Drotter and John Prescott, *The Succession Pipeline: How to Get the Talent You Need When You Need It* (Carlsbad: Motivational Press, 2018), 255.

28 Stephen Drotter and John Prescott, *The Succession Pipeline: How to Get the Talent You Need When You Need It* (Carlsbad: Motivational Press, 2018), 259.

WHAT IS SUCCESSION PLANNING?

- Identification of key roles

- Assessment of performance and potential

- Development

  - By level

  - To fill the gaps

According to The Conference Board's research, the percentage of S&P 500 CEOs reaching retirement age is nearly 17 percent, the highest rate since they began tracking succession.[29] This trend will directly affect organizations' succession planning and test leader readiness. A Harvard Law School report claims, "An aging CEO population is expected to lead to increased leadership turnover, and this phenomenon could rapidly accelerate if the market starts to slow down or reverses its course in the next couple of years. Boards of directors should therefore be aware of the possible surge in the demand for top talent and have a sound CEO succession plan in place to retain a competitive advantage over their peers."[30]

How many organizations are preparing for the definite disruptions, like the aging workforce, and the hypothetical ones, like market disruptions? Not enough. Senior team leaders need to start thinking now about who will fill their leadership roles and ready them for the uncertainties of the future.

---

29 Jason D. Schloetzer, Matteo Tonello, and Gary Larkin, "CEO Succession Practices: 2018 Edition," *The Conference Board*, October 2018, https://www.conference-board.org/publications/publicationdetail.cfm?publicationid=8093.

30 Matteo Tonello and Jason D. Schloetzer, "CEO Succession Practices in the S&P 500," *Harvard Law School Forum on Corporate Governance and Financial Regulation*, October 25, 2018, https://corpgov.law.harvard.edu/2018/10/25/ceo-succession-practices-in-the-sp-500/.

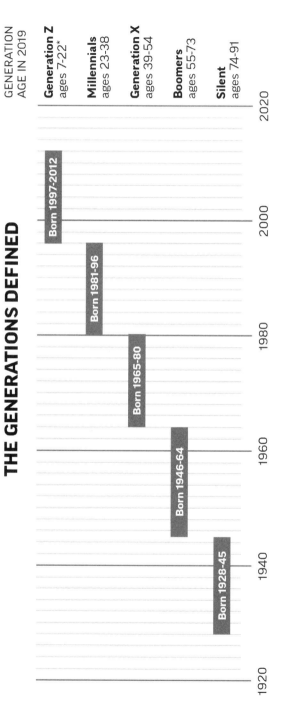

THE GENERATIONS DEFINED

GENERATION AGE IN 2019	
Generation Z	ages 7-22*
Millennials	ages 23-38
Generation X	ages 39-54
Boomers	ages 55-73
Silent	ages 74-91

Born 1997-2012

Born 1981-96

Born 1965-80

Born 1946-64

Born 1928-45

1920   1940   1960   1980   2000   2020

*No chronological endpoint has been set for this group. For this analysis, Generation Z is defined as those ages 7-22 in 2019.

PEW RESEARCH CENTER

MILLENNIALS BECAME THE LARGEST GENERATION IN THE LABOR FORCE IN 2016

U.S. labor force, in millions

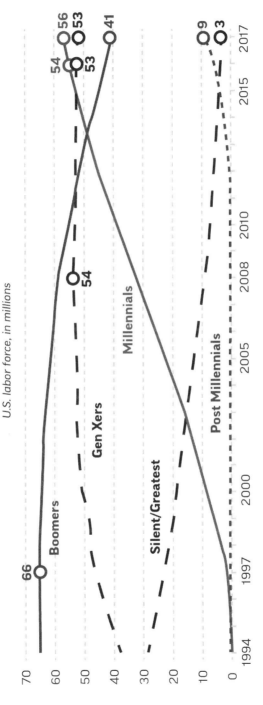

Note: Labor force includes those ages 16 and older who are working or looking for work. Annual averages shown.
Source: Pew Research Center analysis of monthly 1994-2017 Current Population Survey (IPUMS).

PEW RESEARCH CENTER

Who will fill these leadership roles? According to the US Census Bureau, millennials are on the cusp of surpassing baby boomers as the nation's largest living adult generation. In fact, 35 percent of the labor force participants are millennials, which makes them the largest generation working today.[31] This means that 56 million millennials are actively working or looking for work.[32] The problem, however, is despite the size of the millennial labor force, it will not reach the size of the baby boomer labor force, which peaked at 66 million in 1997.[33] This translates to a crisis in leadership pipelines across markets and industries. There will be no avoiding this crisis. The only way to weather it will be early foresight and planning of senior leaders.

The reality is that we don't have enough people rising up to successfully assume the place of boomers in today's environment, and millennials and Generation Z employees aren't equipped to take over for older generations because the standard education and training systems are lacking. Furthermore, according to my decades of observations, we are giving them less time to prepare for each increase in responsibility than we have historically.

We used to have longer amounts of time to prepare emerging leaders. With the traditional succession plan, you might be at your supervisor's knee for ten years learning. The world wasn't moving as fast; there was more time to develop people. More time for development meant there were more choices and more competition. CEOs could pick the best of the best. Traditionally, a CEO would see potential in a few emerging leaders, for example, and spend time grooming each of them. Inevitably, one would emerge as the top

---

31   Richard Fry, "Millennials are the largest generation in the U.S. labor force," *Pew Research Center*, April 11, 2018, https://www.pewresearch.org/fact-tank/2018/04/11/millennials-largest-generation-us-labor-force/.

32   Ibid.

33   Ibid.

candidate. Now, they can't find anyone to nominate, so they either choose someone who is not ready, or they pick several potential candidates and wait years to develop them properly. Since it's rare that an organization can put off their succession for years, their only other option is to bring in leaders from the outside.

Professor and author Noel Tichy argues that "every time an organization's board needs to reach outside its own ranks for a successor … such a desperate move, even if at the time it may be hailed as a breakthrough, is in fact an unmistakable sign of a broken leadership pipeline, and in my experience, broken leadership pipelines are the primary root cause of broken companies."[34]

Not only do external hires point to larger systemic problem within organizations, but they also set it up for failure. A study by Matthew Bidwell, a professor at the Wharton School, examined six years of data covering nearly 5,300 employees from varying positions. He found that despite being paid 18 percent to 20 percent more than internal employees for the same position, they score lower on performance reviews during their first two years; not only were they more expensive, but they were also 61 percent more likely to be laid off or fired and 21 percent more likely to leave their job, compared to their internal counterparts.[35] As you can see, planning to hire from outside the organization is costly and less effective. We must shore up the leadership pipeline

Leadership development is more urgent now than ever. You can't keep doing things the way they've always been done because we are entering a new phase of limited leaders.

---

34 Noel Tichy, *Succession: Mastering the Make-or-Break Process of Leadership Transition* (New York: Portfolio, 2014), 20.

35 Matthew Bidwell, "Paying More to Get Less: The Effects of External Hiring Versus Internal Mobility," *Administrative Science Quarterly* 56, no. 3 (2011): 369–407.

so we have in-house candidates ready to take the lead.

Leadership development is more urgent now than ever. You can't keep doing things the way they've always been done because we are entering a new phase of limited leaders. If we have to count on the millennials, in particular, they're not going to be ready, because we're not intentionally developing them in the right way. That leaves us with some qualified leaders at the top doing way more than they need to do because that's what they "have" to do. Or they're putting young people into situations they're not prepared for. That's stressful at best and fails at worst. That's a lot of pressure on leaders who may not be developed or supported properly.

SHIFTING EXPECTATIONS IN THE WORKPLACE

In addition to emerging technologies, industry fluctuations, and the impending shortage of leaders, we will soon be grappling with the expectations of our upcoming leaders. The generations that will be tasked with filling leadership roles—mainly the millennials and Generation Z—have different outlooks than previous ones.

According to a global study of these two generations, they have vastly different workplace expectations than those of the past. First, they are skeptical of the business world's motives; only 55 percent of those polled said business has a positive impact on society, which is down from the 61 percent reported in 2018.[36] Young generations tend to be more mobile as well, with more young people than ever—49 percent—reporting they would quit their current jobs in the next two years if given the choice.[37] Even more alarming might be the way they view business leaders, with only 37 percent believing

---

36   "The Deloitte Global Millennial Survey 2019," *Deloitte*, https://www2.deloitte. com/global/en/pages/about-deloitte/articles/millennialsurvey.html.

37   Ibid.

they make a positive impact on the world and 26 percent reporting they don't trust leaders for reliable information.[38]

With this much skepticism in our emerging leaders, we need even stronger senior leaders who can share a vision of opportunity to excite and inspire them. Millennials and members of Generation Z need to feel safe and secure in their working environments, and it's today's senior leaders who need to be responsible for this.

Another problem that will emerge as these generations transition into vacant leadership roles is that only about one in five believe they have the skills and knowledge they'll need for a world being shaped by new trends in automation and data exchange.[39] Furthermore, 70 percent report they may only have some or few of the working skills required.[40] This demonstrates how much emerging leaders will rely on their senior leaders and organizational development professionals to ready them for the chaotic markets into which they're entering. Since they don't feel ready for leadership themselves, millennials reported they hold others accountable to prepare them—30 percent said businesses held the greatest responsibility to train them; 24 percent said educational institutions.[41] As we've discussed, if current leadership development and standard educational training is failing emerging leaders, then who will ready them?

Another trend in younger generations is their emphasis on experiences. In addition to higher expectations, the younger generations are more self-aware than others. They seek innovation and productivity, and in some ways seem more goal oriented than previous ones. In fact, some researchers are saying these generations are more entrepre-

---

38   Ibid.

39   Ibid.

40   Ibid.

41   Ibid.

neurial than ever, with 62 percent reporting they would like to start their own companies rather than work for established businesses.[42] The only difference? Their goals have changed. Rather than settling down in a nice house with a nice job, 57 percent reported that travel was their top aspiration, and only 49 percent said they wanted to own a home.[43]

This research shows that organizations are going to be held accountable in new ways. Younger generations are choosing and adopting their own mindset rather than having what's handed down to them. They want to be engaged in their workplace. They want to make a difference. They want a clear line of sight to understand how they fit into the company's larger mission outside of revenue. They want to feel appreciated and have resources to do their jobs well. They are also making choices that are not driven by money. They prefer flexibility, positive workplace culture, and engagement opportunities. It's not going to be enough to give them a salary and ignore these other factors. Organizations will be held accountable in new ways to meet the higher expectations of tomorrow's leaders. The time to prepare is now.

WHO HAS GOTTEN IT RIGHT?

Changes are imminent in our leadership forces. You can count on that. If you continue to use the standard leadership development, this new group of young leaders who value experience and engagement will not last long at your organization. They will find places that value them

---

42   Marcie Merriman, "What if the next big disruptor isn't a *what* but a *who*?" Ernst & Young LLP, 2015, https://www.ey.com/Publication/vwLUAssets/EY-rise-of-gen-znew-challenge-for-retailers/%24FILE/EY-rise-of-gen-znew-challenge-for-retailers.pdf.

43   "The Deloitte Global Millennial Survey 2019," *Deloitte*, https://www2.deloitte.com/global/en/pages/about-deloitte/articles/millennialsurvey.html.

and have systems in place to support and develop them.

Companies like GE, Marriott, IBM, General Mills, and Procter & Gamble have become pioneers in the leadership development world, and their continued success shows how investing in your people is also investing in your viability. The fact that these pioneers in leadership development are also household names say a lot about their successes. Some companies value their leaders so much, in fact, that they have created leadership institutes. I'm not saying that every organization needs an institute, but I do think we need to look closely at how they are prioritizing their leaders if we are to duplicate their achievements.

Much of GE's accomplishments can be credited to its corporate learning facility in Crotonville, New York. In the mid-1950s, GE's president, Ralph Cordiner, determined that his company's biggest threat was its managers. At this time, GE was experiencing rapid growth, and without a competent roster of managers to rely on, he saw this could limit their potential. He decided to try an innovative approach to readying his future leaders. The first seminar held at the management training center was thirteen weeks long. (I know *that* would surely illicit some eye rolls and exasperated sighs.) Though it sounds like an absurdly long development course, it worked, and it produced one of its future CEOs, Reginald Jones.

Since that time, the global leadership institute has now developed more than forty thousand participants. Its courses are typically two-week sessions held on its fifty-nine-acre campus. In an interview with the Wharton School, former chief learning officer Susan Peters said, "The mission of our leadership effort is to inspire, connect, and develop the leaders of today and tomorrow. That is our objective … If we do a good job with the people who come through the Crotonville classes, there is a huge multiplier effect. They go back and hopefully do the same thing—inspire, connect, and develop the people who work for them."[44]

Granted, GE does spend a whopping $1 billion a year in training, which is unrealistic for most organizations. We can, however, see what they are getting right about leadership: they're being proactive. They don't wait until they are in a succession crisis, for example, to value leadership. They stay ahead of issues and fix them before they're broken. Next, they start training early. They begin developing their leaders before they place them in the roles. Furthermore, they transfer knowledge to leaders in a way they can put it in play more easily. They're giving them what they need, when they need it, at the appropriate level. Their teachings are also tied to their strategic initiatives. When all of these factors combine, it creates effective programs that the employees are excited to attend because they are engaged in their own development. I have interviewed several people who have attended these programs, and they can artfully define what leadership is, and they understand it's a big part of their job.

Raghu Krishamoorthy, GE's senior VP of Global HR—and former VP of executive development and chief learning officer—says the success of their leadership development is because it comes from the highest leadership level so that the right people are in the right program:[45]

> At GE, each of our eight big businesses has assigned a very
> senior leader who either heads a function or a business to

---

44   Susan Peters, "How GE Builds Global Leaders: A Conversation with Chief Learning Officer Susan Peters." *Wharton*, May 12, 2010. Transcript. https://knowledge.wharton.upenn.edu/article/how-ge-builds-global-leaders-a-conversation-with-chief-learning-officer-susan-peters/.

45   Raghu Krishamoorthy, "How GE Trains More Experienced Employees," *Harvard Business Review*, May 16, 2014, https://hbr.org/2014/05/how-ge-trains-more-experienced-employees.

be the sponsor of the mid-career programs. The sponsors ensure that the right candidates from the business are hired into each program, and they play a key role in ensuring that the participants get the most challenging assignments. They also see to it that the off-program assignment for the individual does justice to the investment in the individual. Such sponsorship ensures visibility and credibility of those in the program and positions them well with assignment leaders.

Krishamoorthy also highlights that their program works because they garner continuous 360-degree feedback and maintain close assignment coaching. By ensuring there is constant feedback and coaching to develop the proper behavior, they create an integrated, experiential opportunity for development. These are exactly the kinds of experiences millennials and members of Generation Z will be seeking. If you are not offering them within your own organization, they will find places that do.

Companies like GE, which have invested time, money, and value into the development of their leaders, are more prepared for the chaos and disruptions in markets and industries. Despite the transitions they might experience, they have a roster of managers who have been developed for leadership. This means they are positioned to remain robust organizations that can withstand whatever changes might occur.

WHY NOW?

At the end of the Cold War, the US Army War College described the world as being more volatile, uncertain, complex, and ambiguous (VUCA). The VUCA concept has gained relevance in the business world and is often used to describe the skills needed in current and emerging leaders. The VUCA environment will continue to demand learning and adaptation, so leaders who aren't prepared put their teams and organizations at risk.

Thanks to the internet, mobile technology, social platforms, and constant industry innovations, we can expect a disrupted, chaotic environment to continue. This is the new normal. Furthermore, our senior leaders will be retiring, and we will need new leaders to fortify our organizations. Business will either evolve and learn to thrive amid the changes, or they will become extinct.

Using recent research in business and technology, Leah Jonson, vice president of Gartner—a leading research and advisory company—says, "HR's priorities in 2020 reflect the urgent need to get out ahead of today's uncertain operating conditions. Digital transformation has already been creating gaps in skills and straining the capabilities of leadership. Now we see that organizations also lack the expertise needed to restructure their organizations and manage the change that is washing over every organization."[46] Her metaphor is apt: the changes ahead are like a tsunami. You can't eradicate it, but you can prepare for it through strategic planning and proactive leader development.

Technology will continue to advance at a breakneck pace, making it increasingly harder to keep up. Considering that we already struggle to respond to texts, emails, tweets, and calls, this will only increase the burden and time restraints our leaders feel. All of these factors combined lead to chaos, and without proper development, leaders won't be able to keep up. As the demand continues to grow, there will be fewer leaders relative to the number of roles available,

---

46 Jackie Wiles, "Gartner Top 3 Priorities for HR Leaders in 2020," *Gartner*, November 18, 2019. https://www.gartner.com/smarterwithgartner/ gartner-top-3-priorities-for-hr-leaders-in-2020/.

as we saw in this chapter's opening example. We can count on the changes, but we cannot count on leaders being ready to handle them.

Chaos in the marketplace and world is going to affect everybody. Many economic advisers predicted another downturn similar to 2008, and we are looking at an unprecedented financial downturn as I write this book. What does that mean for leadership development? Usually when economic upheaval happens, CEOs either pull back on spending, or they don't do anything at all and wait for the chaos to pass. During a downturn, CEOs don't have the budget to do anything extraneous, and unfortunately leadership development often falls under this category. There would be no more development classes or off-sites. Senior leaders would seek efficient, pared-down leadership development, if they sought it at all.

Even though some CEOs hide, there is another path that allows CEOs to capitalize on economic disruptions. If they are clever and innovative, they will focus on developing people when the economy recesses. They will understand the advantage it provides them on the back end. While other senior leaders are letting people go to cut costs, successful leaders keep moving ahead to ensure their organization can counter the chaotic environment and double down on people. Where will leaders want to go at the end of a recession when only a few companies are investing in their people?

When the markets are disrupted, you need strong leadership more than ever. The chaos that can take other organizations down can actually leverage some companies into their most profitable times, as evidenced by development behemoths like GE. An effective leader has to be able to sort through what's hitting them at once and prioritize the right things that add the highest value. They have to stop doing certain tasks and start helping others execute those tasks. Having a team of leaders putting this into play can be the difference between your organization's evolution to the next level or its extinction. The choice is up to you and your leadership development plans.

If it's always been broken, why fix it now? Because if it's not fixed now, our leaders will fail, and then their teams and businesses will follow. With the frenzied pace of the current business world—and the world at large—we are putting more pressure and responsibilities on our executives. This will undoubtedly lead to burnout. In fact, many colleagues have shared with me that if they had known how challenging their field or their role would become, they never would have taken the job. They are overworked, overstressed, and overextended. We must heed these complaints as a warning and support our leaders today so we can depend on our teams tomorrow.

You can put off developing leaders for another month, year, decade, but your business will suffer. You will waste money and time with the training you do provide. Your most costly resource is likely your people, and without effective leadership, you aren't getting the most out of your priciest resource. If your business is struggling in any area, look to your people and the leaders who are tasked with developing and supporting them. If your business is failing, it's because your people are failing.

> *If your business is failing, it's because your people are failing.*

One of the most common complaints I hear from CEOs is, "The business is fine right now, but I don't think the team can take it to the next level." Don't wait until your business is suffering to strengthen your teams. CEOs spend decades building businesses, only to watch them fail because there is no one on the bench who is prepared to get in the game.

Part of the reason why leadership development must evolve is because leadership has evolved. The traditional leader used to be an autocratic one who barked, "This is what we're doing. This is how we do it. Go do it!" We are in a different place now; we have different information, and we have a new generation of leaders with distinctive expectations and priorities.

The impacts are detrimental if we don't change the way we develop leaders. Evidence suggests that of the $200 billion spent annually in the United States from training and development, barely 10 percent delivers results.[47] Considering that it's not working in its current form for most companies, this is an incredible waste. It is my hope that organizational development professionals will realize that leaders deserve better.

As we will explore in Part II, there are innovative ways to deliver and absorb information, and when these skills are consistently adopted, they have been proven to work. When your leadership development practices evolve as leaders evolve, the gains are huge. If you are a senior leader, you've got to consider this now because once your competitors do, they will get ahead of you. Then, not only will you have wasted money, but your upcoming leaders also won't be prepared for what the future holds at your company—and in the world at large.

---

47   Mihnea Moldoveanu and Das Narayandas, "The Future of Leadership Development," *Harvard Business Review*, March–April 2019, https://hbr.org/2019/03/educating-the-next-generation-of-leaders.

PART II

WHAT'S THE SOLUTION?

CHAPTER 4

The Four Drivers of Leader Development Success

For more than twenty years, I have worked with a regional hospital system we'll call AHS, which employs more than thirteen hundred employees across over two hundred locations. During that time, I have witnessed monumental changes within AHS itself and within the healthcare industry at large. Their most pressing problem was that, despite the industry's growth, AHS did not have leaders ready to handle the constantly changing environment. There were signs of burnout in all areas, and the leaders recognized they could not handle the volume of what was undoubtedly coming their way. Aim, fire … aim, fire … all day long.

AHS's internal leadership development team was comprised of four people who were charged with running development for an entire organization—including clinicians. When we asked them what they wanted their leaders to be able to do broadly, they had varying answers. We asked what outcomes they desired from their current programs, and they cited "general readiness" for leaders. As for their current development programs, they couldn't name any results. Despite how logical it seems to be able to answer these general questions, their responses—or lack thereof—remain quite common.

The company did have quite a few development programs in place, but it was a haphazard mix of information cobbled together reactively over time as new needs arose. As they added content in, though, they didn't filter any out. This went on year after year, never being questioned. Eventually, they ended up with piecemeal programs that weren't focused on their team's current needs. For example, the chief nursing officer decided that in order for nurses to become leaders, they needed to be able to read financial statements. It's certainly not a bad thing to learn how to read a financial statement; in fact, it's quite helpful. The problem resided in their failure to connect this new skill to the employees' jobs and the company's overall mission. Lapses like these weakened their leaders and teams and squashed leaders' excitement in their own development. Their leaders deserved better.

Leadership development is not a secret formula to be discovered. It's often much simpler than that. For AHS, the four people on the leadership development team did not understand what was working, what wasn't working, where they wanted to go, or how they were going to get there. Furthermore, despite spending $2 million on developmental efforts per year, the company kept offering the same programs they always had, so readiness of leaders became a wide chasm that inhibited their growth and potential—fatal flaws for any business.

> *Leadership development is not a secret formula to be discovered. It's often much simpler than that.*

AHS focused on a lot of the right things—they had tightened their processes and offered quality care—but they "didn't have time" to develop their future leaders, nor did they think their current approached needed changing. Being in the healthcare industry, they understood that their ability to weather change was a predictor of their viability. Even though they were doing "okay" financially, they had the foresight to understand their failure to develop tomorrow's leaders put them at great risk. As AHS learned, they could still be successful despite their challenges, but they were more painful, hard-fought successes that were wearing out their people and their processes in the meantime.

Unfortunately, the challenges AHS experienced are not limited to one company or one industry. According to the Conference Board's 2019 global study of CEOs, the top external concern recognized by the polled CEOs was recession, and the top internal concern was talent retention and leader development.[48] Why talent? Because CEOs know that strong people are absolutely vital to the bottom line. If a company is failing, you can always trace that failure back to its people, and vice versa. The problem for AHS, and common problems for many businesses and organizations, was that they didn't know *why* what they had in place wasn't working, and they didn't know *how* to fix it. That's why I offered them a solution that harnessed the Four Drivers of Leader Development Success.

THE FOUR DRIVERS OF LEADER DEVELOPMENT SUCCESS

From experience, I have determined there are Four Drivers of Leader Development Success that are essential components of effective

---

48 The Conference Board, "In 2019, CEOs are Most Concerned About Talent and a Recession," *PR Newswire,* January 17, 2019, https://www.prnewswire.com/news-releases/in-2019-ceos-are-most-concerned-about-talent-and-a-recession-300779592.html.

people development. They are proven components, and a plan must incorporate each one in order to deliver effectual outcomes.

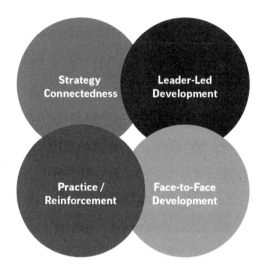

1. The Overarching People Strategy Must Be Connected to the Business Strategy

Connecting people strategy to business strategy doesn't alter *how* you develop people; rather, it's concerned with *why* you develop people and *how* you measure success. The content may be the same, but the change is that the leadership team, human resources, and the people to be developed all understand the overall strategy. All involved must know where the business is headed so they can determine how their leadership development will get them where they want to go. Participants need to see that their development will further the larger goal. When the senior leaders can see it, they are more likely to invest money; when participants can see it, they are more likely to retain the knowledge and put it in play because they understand what they're charged with and where they add value; when HR people can see it, they are more likely to design the right programs to get everyone there.

2. Leadership Development Must Be Leader-Led

Leaders can teach other leaders and direct reports how to do their respective jobs, reducing the need for some formal development, and can provide employees with a sense of purpose and potential. Whether you are a leader of leaders or a leader of others, it is your responsibility to lead development.

Leaders of others must understand their primary role is to develop individual contributors, and they must do this daily. They need to be abreast of what individual contributors require to do their jobs well and how to support them in their roles. The same goes for leaders of leaders. They have to make sure leaders of others are being developed and getting better, but they also need to understand that what leaders of others need is different than what individual contributors need.

As we will discuss fully in chapter 6, if leaders all understand what's needed at each level of leadership, then they can develop their direct reports in the right way. No matter the leadership level, leaders need to know what makes an individual successful and work to develop that. If leaders are executing this on a daily basis, they may not need outside help to develop people.

3. Leaders Must Be Able to Put into Play the Skills They Learn

Senior leaders and leaders of leaders must remove barriers that get in the way of leaders incorporating new skills into their current work—like a boss whose expectations don't change and whose evaluations don't incorporate the new learning, or a direct report who returns to daily tasks without an understanding of how to practice their newly acquired skills. We need to measure what matters, and that includes the way leaders are developing others. After all, that's their key role.

If measured competencies aren't tied to what individual contributors are learning, they don't seem to matter. This is why the people they report to need to support the development and why successful leadership programs begin in conversations with senior leaders about their objectives. Leaders of participants must understand the programs and receive guidelines on how to support direct reports.

After development, most participants want to put their new skills into practice, but oftentimes there are barriers in place that prevent them—maybe their boss isn't supportive, or the skills are not tied to employee evaluations. This can be remedied by holding a separate meeting post-training to discuss the action plans cohorts received during development and how they plan to implement the pieces they learned. As we will discuss fully in chapter 7, it's vital that leaders are involved, supportive, and prepared to hold participants accountable.

4. Leadership Development Must Have Face-to-Face Components

Digital learning has a host of applications for which it can be effective; leadership development, however, is not one of them. Everybody wants digital learning to work because it's convenient and cheaper than face-to-face. In an ideal world, technology would lead the way in leaders learning, but in the real world, it doesn't.

Developing leaders needs to be in person, at the participant's level. When you need participants to have overarching leadership skills, where it's more interpersonal, collaborative, and includes more "people stuff," you have to do this work in person—though you can augment the development on the front end and back end with information on an app or online. As we will explore in later chapters, people need to be together to effectively learn from each other.

Let's look at how Oliver Group applied the Four Drivers of Leader Development Success to create an effective development strategy for the people of AHS.

THE FOUR DRIVERS OF LEADER DEVELOPMENT SUCCESS AT WORK

When Oliver Group consulted with AHS, we first compared their current leadership development against the Four Drivers of Leader Development Success.

1. The Overarching People Strategy Must Be Connected to the Business Strategy

AHS's people strategy wasn't connected to their business strategy, and that's why they had a hodgepodge of ineffective programs. The fluxes in the healthcare industry further tested their ability to connect people with business strategies. Instead of capturing outcomes, they were forced to rely on patient metrics: satisfaction, length of stay, incidents margin, and more. This did not give them ways to gauge their leaders and their future readiness.

In order to connect AHS's people strategy to its business strategy, we had to first discuss what *strategy* means. Despite it being a commonly used word in the industry, few can define what it is. Oftentimes my clients assume their business strategy is the same as their financial goal. In reality, however, strategy encompasses much more than that. A strategy is incomplete unless it accounts for people, processes, clients/customers, and financial pieces. The organization is unbalanced without this full picture. Furthermore, it must also consider an organization's mission, vision, values, strategies, goals, and tactics, which we will explore fully in chapter 5.

When AHS was creating their strategies, they had to take into consideration the current and future states of their people, processes, clients/customers, and finances, and identify the gaps between them. Once we connected AHS's people strategy to its business strategy, we had to move to the next Driver of Leader Development Success: *Leadership development must be leader-led.*

2. Leadership Development Must Be Leader-Led

Leadership development at AHS was provided by internal and external facilitators about a variety of topics. Senior leaders were not involved in the development at all. Understandably, this created a chasm between those developed and their leaders.

In an effort to achieve leader-led development, senior leaders were included in the pilot program to show buy-in and to understand what their leaders were learning. They needed leaders to be ready. In the further rollout, we asked that all AHS leaders participate in a version of the pilot within two to three years. Once all leaders attended the right program for their level, they knew how to provide an ongoing learning environment. One goal for these teams was to make sure they understood how to work—and that they were working—at the level their role required.

The foundation of the pilot program was rooted in the concept of leader transitions: that a leader could not progress to the next level without having mastered the work values, time application, and skills associated with their current level. Failure to do this could clog the pipeline and negatively affect engagement and performance of teams, which have well-researched financial impacts. In fact, organizations that successfully engage their employees "realize substantially better customer engagement, higher productivity, better retention, fewer accidents, and 21 percent higher profitability."[49]

Additionally, if a leader of leaders was not performing at their level, it could drag down their direct report's ability to grow and learn the next level of competencies because the leader of leaders

---

49 Jim Harter, "Employee Engagement on the Rise in the U.S.," *Gallup*, August 26, 2018, https://news.gallup.com/poll/241649/employee-engagement-rise.aspx.

is doing their direct report's job. Ultimately the ability to function effectively at the next level will be impeded. To continue to foster the leader-led approach, meetings between leaders and direct reports were established to review data, validate growth goals, and establish interactive cadence between the leader and executive throughout the learning journey.

3. Leaders Must Be Able to Put into Play the Skills They Learn

This was not happening at AHS. They did not put skills into their performance reviews, into their job descriptions, or into their expectations. For example, after development, they went back to what they knew—being physicians who take care of patients. Leadership didn't become part of their practice, and thus, it didn't stick.

In order to create the soundest leadership development, we had to acknowledge the Third Driver of Leader Development Success: *Leaders must be able to put into play the skills they learn.* During this phase, we focused on the execution of the skills, and it involved the real-life application of new behaviors and competencies learned and practiced during the immersion in the workshop. It also involved regular check-ins with Oliver Group to ensure the work remained relevant and adaptive, and to enable concrete conversations around visible change taking place among the leaders. This intentional application of learning determined the level of growth among each leader.

4. Leadership Development Must Have Face-to-Face Components

Unlike many organizations, AHS didn't participate in a lot of digital training. Instead, they offered most development face-to-face, which is ideal. Though AHS had one of the Four Drivers in place, it wasn't enough to bolster the leadership development. In order to create effective programs, it is crucial that you harness all of the Four Drivers. Like cogs in a wheel, each one is needed to keep the process moving. When one is missing, the wheel can't turn, and it affects the entire machine's function.

To elevate their existing programs, we created workshop sessions in which the leaders came together and were immersed in highly interactive and dynamic learning formats around leadership principles and competencies. The workshop was designed around a proven adult-learning model and follows the 70/20/10 rule: 70 percent is actual, real-life learning demonstrated through simulation and role play around real leader issues, 20 percent is shared knowledge gained from peer interaction, and only 10 percent is facilitator lecture to impart key concepts.

It is crucial that you harness all of the Four Drivers. Like cogs in a wheel, each one is needed to keep the process moving.

This phase also included cycles of self-assessment to regauge the knowledge, application, and attitude of the leader toward the concepts practiced in the workshop. We also established cohort coaching sessions. As with any behavioral change, adoption is directly related to repetition and practice. Oliver Group designed the program to include coaching after the sessions. This consisted of peer-led group coaching once per month and facilitator-led group coaching once per month. Group coaching not only drove further accountability for change and action, but it also created more transparency and support among the leaders as they grappled with similar issues. Additionally, the coach was available for one-off calls for specific issues, clarification, and situational support.

CONCLUSION

With our guidance using the Four Drivers, AHS's senior leadership team identified that developing talent was one of their most critical short-term focus areas, while continuing to promote growth and guard against business performance challenges comprised their long-term focus. They also aimed to provide more clear succession readiness, to grow the leadership capacity for the organization, and to tie the development to measured company performance. Lastly, they planned for development to prepare women and minorities for future leadership roles.

Based on the proven history and the strength of the Four Drivers, Oliver Group brought a unique and tailored approach to the development of leadership talent at AHS while promoting long-term growth and guarding against cultural and business performance challenges.

So, now that we understand how the Four Drivers of Leader Development Success work together, let's look at each one closer so business leaders can evaluate their current development and begin transforming into something their leaders deserve.

CHRISTOPHER GRIFFIN, PRESIDENT AND CEO OF USG, ON LEADERSHIP:

At USG, I'm fortunate because we are 117 years old with mature and robust processes around talent development and succession planning. This makes it easier to gauge how we're doing and see where we are.

There are several factors to consider when working with HR leaders and learning and development leaders to create continuity between development strategy. One of the challenges with any organization is getting people to give me feedback. I'm genuinely interested in how my leaders are feeling. If I've talked to a group of employees, I ask, "Are there things that I could have done better? Was I on message? What did I do well? What did I not do well?" In truth, it takes a while for people to be comfortable giving you that feedback because it's not traditional. People always want to show respect and are cautious to give a superior feedback. I've found, however, that feedback is absolutely critical if we're going to be a team together.

When it comes to clearly defining a development strategy, the responsibility falls to those of us at the top of any organization. We have to ask: *What does winning look like? Why is that good for the company? How do we communicate that to every individual in the organization? How do we make those connections? Why do people come to work every day? Why do they come to work and want to participate and help us?* This strategy can't be designed just to be good for the company; it has to be good for each employee personally.

Defining a development strategy is really about helping leaders understand that their power is not about making themselves 10 percent more productive or 15 percent better. It's about making them better coaches to the ten or fifteen people they lead to make those direct reports 10 or 15 percent better. We want to create a multiple effect across the organization.

The real challenge is practicing effective questioning every day. You can imagine how many times a day somebody might walk into your office with a problem wanting you to solve it. How do you resist the temptation to give the answer and not use effective questioning to help them develop the answer? In the short term, a lot of people might want to hear the answer done and move on. In the long term, however, if your goal is to develop the person, you want them to have the skill to come to the answer on their own. That's leadership. Sometimes you might even want to let them fail. If they've come to an answer that might not be the answer that you would have given, are you prepared to let them take a different path? They might be successful, but they also might fail. Those are difficult things to allow in the environment in which we operate today. Giving people permission to risk failure is a difficult challenge.

I often joke that I don't make anything and I don't sell anything. Therefore, the only value I provide to the organization is getting the resources so that others can be successful. That's it. This is why I need my teams to be effective. If they're effective, I'm successful. It's as simple as that.

CHAPTER 5

Align to Alive

Along-standing client, NISC, is a privately held co-op that implements and supports software and hardware for their members in telecom and utilities. In their early years, NISC had strong, but not fast, growth. Because the pace of the industry was slower at that time, however, they had more time to prepare people. Unfortunately, they didn't know how to structure that time, so they taught themselves how to be good leaders by reading, observing other good leaders, and learning hands-on from mistakes. Development was haphazard and informal, but the company focused more on software development than people; leadership was an afterthought to getting the software right.

Due to the changes going on in utility and telecom industries, information technology had become an even more important issue, and NISC experienced a lot of growth as a result. In fact, they hired 250 people in 2019 alone. With their burgeoning growth, they started to suffer from not having leaders prepared. They saw they had a gap—not in selling their product—but in hiring and developing enough talent to meet the customer demands. Furthermore, 80 percent of their new hires were right out of universities, so prepared leaders were more critical to NISC with these novice workers to bring in their fold and develop. Their pulse survey showed that leaders were struggling to provide employees what they needed. They required strong leadership, and they needed it *now*.

NISC was on the cusp of several transitions. The first was that their CEO—who had been at NISC for forty-five of the company's fifty years—was preparing for retirement. In 2009, the president and CEO, Vern Dosch, realized succession was a problem and looked at all positions to see if they had people ready one year out, three years out, and five years out. Unfortunately, the people they wanted to step up didn't have the experience or skills yet. Dosch realized NISC wasn't ready for him to retire because they didn't have internal candidates ready to take on new leadership roles.

Furthermore, NISC had high numbers of leadership retirements. Of their leaders, an astounding 40 percent would need to be rehired. Because the company was in a rural part of the country, it was oftentimes difficult to entice people to move there. Their best strategy was to hire from within, but few middle managers were ready. They would need to develop people internally in order to keep up their growth. But how?

Initially when Dosch, approached Oliver Group, he said it was because he wanted to "leave a legacy." After discussing his legacy further, he said, "I want this organization set up for success with the right leaders in place at all the right levels." Dosch saw the impending disruptions ahead, and he knew the company's current situation was untenable. The clock was ticking. They had several years to train people to take over successfully and create a legacy they, and Dosch himself, could be proud of.

Because they were a technically oriented business, most of their leaders were also technical in nature, which precluded emphasis on people development. Dosch understood they would need a culture shift in order for the learning development to be successful. They needed to transition from valuing leaders' technical competencies to valuing their ability to prepare those who are less experienced. They leveraged getting programs that were appropriate at all the levels— starting with the senior team. No matter the role in the company, each senior team member needed to understand what a functional leader should focus on. How are they each expected to spend their time? What work should each value the most? And how should they develop their leaders of leaders?

NISC leaders had to determine where they were, where they needed to be in several years, and how they would get there. With Oliver Group's help, they put a program together to address those needs and tie their planning to strategy—which required a much different approach than providing potential leaders with development on miscellaneous topics.

When NISC shared with us the components of their business strategy and the outcomes they were hoping for, we explained the importance of getting the senior team on board first. We wanted to help them see a higher value of the development before we even began. This led to a daylong session with all executive leaders to help them better understand their objectives, their outcomes, and how those connected to their larger people plan. They needed to understand that NISC was investing in each leader for the viability of the organization so senior leaders could continue to promote internally.

Leaders also needed to recognize their role in the plan and what was required of them, so we created four days of development programs for NISC cohorts around the key areas identified by senior leaders. We devised measures for those leaders and created a heat map to show how leaders were doing in developing all competencies. Along the way, we checked in to see whether the information was retained and their behaviors were changing. Every group improved, so NISC continued investing in their development.

After two years of working with Oliver Group, about 90 percent of NISC leaders had been through leadership development programs for the level they currently held. Afterward, leaders understood what was expected of them from a leadership perspective and how that was measured in terms of performance. When we asked NISC what leadership behaviors they were observing across the organization a year after development, they reported the following changes:

- Decision-making and problem-solving were pushed to the appropriate leadership levels.

- There was an increased focus on leadership accountability.

- The senior team was playing an enhanced strategic role.

- The leaders were responsible for a refreshed approach to talent management with specific related performance goals.

NISC understood their goals, and the CEO and the VP of HR worked closely together to achieve them. Dosch found that holding people accountable was critical, especially top leaders. Over time, his own leadership style evolved, and he began having weekly, one-on-one meetings with each of his direct reports, which he had never done before. He said they were overwhelming at first and a big commitment, but the relationship and candid conversations they generated were key to the CEO transition.

They also implemented an annual strategic planning process wherein they focused on several pertinent initiatives, as agreed upon by the board, that included a piece for acquiring and developing people. Furthermore, they created an all-supervisory group, called the Management Communication Group, which met regularly to discuss why they settled on the year's initiatives and what they hoped to accomplish. The goal here was to further encourage buy-in and visibility.

When Dosch announced his retirement ten years after he first realized his succession was problematic, NISC had many external candidates and six internal candidates for his role, which is more than he had hoped for. Ultimately, NISC chose an internal candidate. Dosch understood this would create less disruption for the company going forward. "I feel peaceful," he told me after his retirement announcement, "because the plan is working well with various transitions. The new CEO is stepping up, his role is being filled, and there are new opportunities for many employees."

We all have goals for our businesses. To get there, we have to prepare our people to drive the strategies toward that final destination, like mergers, entering new markets, or creating a matrix organization. For NISC, they now believe they have readiness for whatever is coming their way, which is huge because no one knows the shifts ahead for their customers, utility and telecom markets. Despite the changes ahead, NISC knows they have people who will stick with them and work through any conflicts. They saw firsthand how strategy is better realized with better leaders.

> *We all have goals for our businesses. To get there, we have to prepare our people to drive the strategies toward that final destination.*

THE LINK BETWEEN STRATEGY AND PEOPLE

Many companies spend time and effort expanding their business strategies so they can achieve greater performance. Though strategy is important, many executives are missing the link between the business performance and the people who drive it. In a 2020 study, The Predictive Index concluded that "while having an agreed-upon and well-documented business strategy is mission-critical, business strategies don't execute themselves; people do. Senior leaders can maximize strategic performance by crafting an aligned talent strategy that mobilizes employees to handle the execution themselves."[50]

Understanding this profound connection, you would think that business leaders would invest in their people development, but recent research proves this false. The Predictive Index set out to discover how many companies had a talent strategy and whether that strategy drove business success. They found that most companies did have a business strategy—roughly half had a financial plan—but fewer than four in ten had a development plan in place.[51] Of the 36 percent that had a defined people plan, only 10 percent identified strategy alignment as a top priority.[52]

THE STATE OF TALENT OPTIMIZATION REPORT SHOWS:

- Only 66 percent of companies have a business strategy in place.

- Of those, 30 percent said their business strategies were agreed upon.

---

50 The Predictive Index, "The State of Talent Optimization Report," 2020, 2.

51 The Predictive Index, "The State of Talent Optimization Report," 2020, 12.

52 The Predictive Index, "The State of Talent Optimization Report," 2020, 13.

- This means that 70 percent of existing business strategies might not be agreed upon.[53]

When we consider numbers like these, it's easier to understand what is lacking from our standard development model: synergy. From their study, the Predictive Index concluded that, "If these companies hope to design a workforce of engaged employees who row in the same direction, they must draft a business strategy that all senior leaders agree on."[54] As I mentioned, people development isn't a secret formula, but it does involve leaders and teams, business strategies and people strategies all working together to reach a common goal.

Speaking to this disconnect between business plans and people plans, Marilynn Duker, CEO at Brightview Senior Living suggests this is not a new problem: "Doesn't surprise me at all. That's absolutely been the case for us for 20–25 years. We transitioned from a real estate business to an operating company that has real estate as a necessary component—but fundamentally, our product is our people. We have to have the best people who are totally aligned with our culture and our values in order to be successful."[55]

Despite few CEOs linking their people and business strategies as Duker does, The Predictive Index research shows that specific combinations of talent optimization practices—including aligning talent strategy to business strategy—translated to positive business results for the participants they surveyed. In fact, companies that implemented six of the eleven practices outperformed other companies by 16 percent, had 30 percent lower turnover, and had 34 percent

---

53   The Predictive Index, "The State of Talent Optimization Report," 2020, 58.

55   The Predictive Index, "The State of Talent Optimization Report," 2020, 14.

higher employee performance.[56]

These are enormous differentiators in the market, so why are people plans missing from most organizations' strategies? When I talk to clients about their strategic plan, they often assume I am only talking about the financial strategy. Especially in small and midsize organizations, a strategic plan usually means financial projections and goals. Though financial plans are important, that is only one part of a company's strategy. In order to be successful, strategic plans must address more than the financial component. They must consider four categories: people, processes, clients/customers, and financial.

STRATEGIES FALL UNDER FOUR CATEGORIES

---

56   The Predictive Index, "The State of Talent Optimization Report," 2020, 22–25.

If you only focus on one of these categories, your strategy is incomplete. If you decide, for example, that your organization will enter new markets, you can't stop there. You have to connect that objective to your people. What does a new market arena mean for your people? Maybe you will need five hundred new people or ten new leaders with certain skills to achieve your objective. How do you prepare for that?

Larry Clark, managing director of global learning solutions at Harvard Business Publishing, points out that the reactive approach many organizations take leaves them with a hodgepodge of strategies that are disconnected: "With all the programs we are asked to implement to address specific gaps, alongside all the long-standing legacy programs that no one would ever consider pausing, our leadership development strategies may look like a patchwork quilt that displays a fuzzy picture of our organizations' histories and current pain points all mixed together, instead of the purposeful paths they need to be."[57]

As Clark points out, too often CEOs and senior leaders put their people at the bottom of their strategic plans and fail to connect their business strategies to their people strategies. People are part of the plan; in fact, they are the most integral component of your strategies. People victories are business victories, and thus, people strategy and business strategy should be part of the same plan. All businesses would agree that people are important, but that's

> *People victories are business victories, and thus, people strategy and business strategy should be part of the same plan.*

57   Larry Clark, "Is Your 'Vision 2020' Leadership Development Strategy On The Path To Success?" *Harvard Business Publishing Corporate Learning,* August 21, 2018, https://www.harvardbusiness.org/is-your-vision-2020-leadership-development-strategy-on-the-path-to-success/.

not enough to align your strategies for success.

There must be a purposeful link between strategy and people. The business strategy is needed to get to the people strategy. Once you have the people strategy, companies can plan for roles they need (making sure the roles match the strategic and people plans), acquire the right talent based on well-defined roles (or assessments), develop leaders to lead and team members to perform, and measure the outcomes and adjust the plan as needed. Finally, as people execute the plan, organizations can expect people results and business results.

CEOs must ask about the readiness of their leaders today and determine how to get them to where they need to be tomorrow. This must start with a plan that compares current state to future state. Start with your business: Where are you today with your business? Where do you want to go? What are the gaps and how are you going to fill those with strategies? Move to your people: Where are we today? Where do we need to be in the future?

Asking these strategic questions in the context of the four categories (people, processes, clients/customers, and finances) is how strategy is developed. The answers to these questions are where your strategies come from and how you can ensure they are all aligned and working in concert.

THE LINK BETWEEN STRATEGY AND PEOPLE

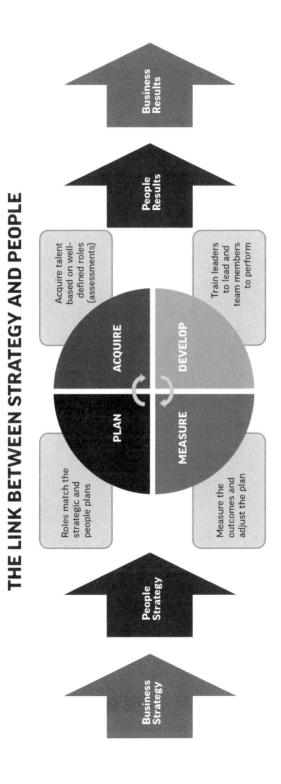

Business Results

People Results

Acquire talent based on well-defined roles (assessments)

Train leaders to lead and team members to perform

ACQUIRE

DEVELOP

PLAN

MEASURE

Roles match the strategic and people plans

Measure the outcomes and adjust the plan

People Strategy

Business Strategy

STRATEGIC QUESTIONS TO ASK FOR EACH OF THE FOUR AREAS: PEOPLE, PROCESSES, CLIENTS/CUSTOMERS, AND FINANCES:

- What is your current state situation?

- Where's your future state?

- What do you want it to look like?

- What are the gaps?

- What are key foci that address the gaps and get you to the future state?

As Dosch learned at NISC, you have to identify your gaps before you draft a business plan. It's the gaps in knowledge, skills, and abilities that point to what people need. It's the development plan that addresses those gaps. Without identifying the gaps, you won't make much progress. Like filling a boat with rowers, but no oars, you won't have the tools you need to get your people or your business to the destination.

Korn Ferry's *Real World Leadership* global report concluded that "organizations need to identify the kinds of leaders required to execute their strategies and then build their development/recruiting approaches around those profiles. Part of that exercise is to include a greater variety of voices and perspectives in the leadership pipeline."[58] This is how NISC identified that despite the growth of their business in its current state and future states, their people were not prepared for the future state. They were then better positioned to create a

---

58 "How to Develop Leaders Who Can Drive Strategic Change," *Harvard Business Review*, March 28, 2017. https://hbr.org/sponsored/2017/03/how-to-develop-leaders-who-can-drive-strategic-change.

business strategy that was aligned with their people strategy.

What does it mean to have a people plan strategy?

- The business plan is understood for the next one to three years.

- Broad strategies for people have been identified to be ready to execute the business plan.

- There's a plan for succession for all key roles.

- Based on the strategies, gaps in knowledge, skills, and abilities have been identified.

- There is an overall development plan for the organization's leaders as a whole and for individuals.

When you look at current state of your people and future state of your people, you often discover you don't have the right kinds of people in the right roles. Thinking strategically about your people allows you to hone in on what knowledge, skills, and abilities are needed where. Ideally, the people plan addresses these gaps.

Our consulting relies on assessments to further determine where the gaps are to best prepare succession plans. Once we understand an organization's key roles, we assess the people in those roles using the Predictive Index tools, measuring their behavior/aptitude and cognitive abilities. We also offer to look at emotional intelligence. This is an integral part of informing a succession plan and identifying who's ready for the next level and how we might develop them further. Assessments like this allow us to make decisions about people as objectively as possible. This precludes individual bias and points to what is best for the individual and the company. We can assess where they are now and what their future potential might be.

Assessments also offer more self-awareness for individuals and teams.

It's beneficial to see if individuals collectively understand the strategies and their places within them. It helps them recognize how they're going to be successful together. Then it overlays their behavior with the various strategic directions the organization may take. For example, if they are in growth mode, they need a certain type of leader to get there. Using assessments, they can see their objective and the makeup of their team. Ideally, they overlap; if they don't overlap, the business strategies aren't aligned with the people strategies. This allows a company to develop leaders with certain capabilities to thrive in a growing market.

When your company goes through tumultuous times or periods of exponential growth, you've got to be able to translate your business strategy to every person and their role within the plan; that's how you align your strategies. Furthermore, it's imperative that everyone involved in the planning and the development believe that they will have a better overall company—with better success—if people are provided what they need.

> *It's imperative that everyone involved in the planning and the development believe that they will have a better overall company—with better success—if people are provided what they need.*

According to HR leaders' responses to the Gartner 2020 *Future of HR* survey, in order to achieve this, senior executives and HR have "to involve employees in co-creating change strategy. Engage the right employees at the right time in the right way—as active participants in making and shaping change decisions."[59] That alignment is a key determinant of whether a company and its strategies will be successful.

---

59   Jackie Wiles, "Gartner Top 3 Priorities for HR Leaders in 2020," *Gartner*, November 18, 2019. https://www.gartner.com/smarterwithgartner/gartner-top-3-priorities-for-hr-leaders-in-2020/.

Once the alignment is determined, it must remain "in sight" for all leaders and their direct reports. This is called line of sight—when the leader knows where the organization is going, and direct reports understand their role in getting there.

BUILDING A CLEAR LINE OF SIGHT

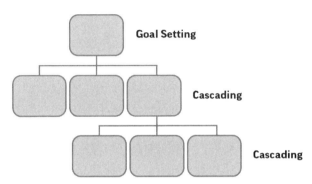

A clear line of sight means that there is a connection between leaders' objectives, the business strategy, and individual contributors' work. Seen from the top of the organization, strategy should be translated into objectives and cascaded clearly down through the organization. In order to have effective people development, a company must have a clear line of sight connected to all the different layers of the organization, and all its people objectives must connect to and support the business strategy.

It is also important for direct reports' engagement and feeling of purpose that they understand exactly how their work and objectives add value to the business. When an individual understands the link between their specific objectives and business strategy, their engagement in the company and its mission grows significantly.

In short, all leaders should be involved in the business and people plans. In *The Succession Pipeline*, authors Drotter and Prescott put much of the responsibility on top-level management to assess "the progress towards delivering the talent needed for achieving business strategy and plans," with business managers evaluating whether the work done addresses the organization's talent needs and lower-level managers focusing on individual and team progress.[60]

Connecting business and people strategies means that, as a leader, you need to discuss the objectives for your indirect reports with your direct reports in order to ensure line of sight. *You* might know what your own objectives are, but to ensure that your direct and indirect reports maintain a clear purpose, they should understand how their work contributes to the value and success of the organization.

ARE YOUR BUSINESS STRATEGIES CONNECTED TO YOUR PEOPLE STRATEGIES?

1. Was HR or leadership development involved alongside the rest of the leadership team in your planning process?

2. Have you identified the roles that are key to your strategy execution?

3. Do you have the right employees in your key roles for strategy execution?

4. Which roles will employees need to be recruited for? What's the recruiting plan?

5. Based on the strategy, will technology significantly change current roles or how work is done?

6. Do you have development plans for key individuals to your strategy? Do you know where to find resources

60 Stephen Drotter and John Prescott, *The Succession Pipeline: How to Get the Talent You Need When You Need It* (Carlsbad: Motivational Press, 2018), 225.

for all developmental needs?

7. What role will leadership play in the implementation of the development plan?

8. What knowledge, skills, or abilities do future leaders need to display? How are these different than those your leaders display today?

9. Do you have the right environment and compensation to attract and retain the top talent you need?

10. Do you have an engaged workforce excited for the upcoming plans? Can your culture drive you toward the future?

Senior leaders have to ensure that people strategy and business strategy are part of the same plan. Essentially, leaders on different levels act as "conduits," connecting the individual to the organization by translating business strategy into relevant objectives and clarifying the link for direct reports. How do they do that? By establishing purpose.

In 1968, one of the nation's leading authorities on education and training, Malcolm Knowles, established a theory to distinguish childhood learning (pedagogy) from adult learning (andragogy), which continues to inform education theories today. Based on his adult learning theory, he found that in order to make learning effective, adult learning has to be purpose driven. Adults need to see the relevance of the material they are learning, and this is why learning needs to be connected to strategy. Knowles determined that adults learn best when material is purpose driven and goal oriented. Writing of Knowles's principles, founder of eLearning Industry's

Network Christopher Pappas says adults have to see "measurable learning objectives and have a clear system of gauging their progress. Otherwise, they'll just walk out of class."[61] Even worse, emerging leaders might walk out of their jobs if they feel they do not understand their role or purpose in an organization.

Authors Drotter and Prescott find that these more abstract concept like engagement and purpose are directly tied to strategic goals and can be indirectly accomplished by focusing on strategy alignment: "Leaders must help align employees to the company's strategic goals—and show them how they can impact those goals. This should build engagement and loyalty; employees go above and beyond when they're emotionally invested in the company's success. When aggregated across the entire workforce, *this* is the differentiator between mediocre and great strategic outcomes. Doing this begins with understanding what drives engagement and disengagement—and acting on that insight."[62]

In addition to engagement, more recent research shows that readying leaders for the challenges of the future remains a top concern for executives. In a survey of 7,500 global leaders, executives cited "accelerating innovation and improving profitability" as one of their top priorities; of those executives surveyed, only 17 percent felt their organizations had "the right leadership to deliver on their strategic business plans."[63] This is why it is critical that executives prioritize the development of leaders who can drive strategic change; otherwise,

---

61   Christopher Pappas, "7 Top Facts About The Adult Learning Theory," *eLearning Industry*, January 20, 2014. https://elearningindustry. com/6-top-facts-about-adult-learning-theory-every-educator-should-know.

62   Stephen Drotter and John Prescott, *The Succession Pipeline: How to Get the Talent You Need When You Need It* (Carlsbad: Motivational Press, 2018), 57.

63   "How to Develop Leaders Who Can Drive Strategic Change," *Harvard Business Review*, March 28, 2017. https://hbr.org/sponsored/2017/03/ how-to-develop-leaders-who-can-drive-strategic-change.

they may be left with no leaders to fill vacancies and drive successes.

Furthermore, more than 50 percent of those surveyed executives ranked their leadership development as "fair" to "very poor"; they also said that if they could start over, they would retain only half of their current leadership development approach.[64] These global numbers show that the problem is not limited to one

It is critical that executives prioritize the development of leaders who can drive strategic change; otherwise, they may be left with no leaders to fill vacancies and drive successes.

industry or one market—it's a universal problem that points to the need for leaders to drive the strategy process. And they will if they are working at their level with the right skills to do so.

BARRIERS TO ALIGNING PEOPLE AND BUSINESS STRATEGIES

There are many ways to garner success, but none is as powerful as strategy alignment. As leadership strategist Josh Bersin notes, strategy alignment is a key indicator of an organization's culture and success:[65]

> Regardless of who the CEO may be, operational execution takes place at the mid-level and supervisory level. When these individuals are well aligned, coached, and trained, the business thrives. High-performing companies understand this, and they build a leadership development program which uniquely trains, supports, and selects people who drive their business's strategy. By doing this,

---

64 Ibid.

65 Josh Bersin, "It's Not The CEO, It's The Leadership Strategy That Matters," *Forbes,* July 30, 2012. https://www.forbes.com/sites/joshbersin/2012/07/30/its-not-the-ceo-its-the-leadership-strategy-that-matters/#2cc65ace6db8.

they build execution into the culture.

If strategy alignment is directly linked to an organization's performance, why do people plans continue to be pushed aside? Because oftentimes the barriers feel insurmountable without sweeping, systemic changes.

BARRIERS TO ALIGNING PEOPLE AND BUSINESS STRATEGIES:

- Lack of support from CEO
- Lack of expertise
- Lack of time and money
- Frequently changing strategies
- HR not valued

One barrier than no one wants to talk about is the CEO's impediment to strategy alignment. Drotter and Prescott calls this a "lack of commitment," and though this is perhaps too kind, they do go on to call this barrier "deadly" to an organization.[66] When a CEO is not invested in his people, the people know. When this happens, Drotter and Prescott place the responsibility on the head of HR, who "must call on the CEO to be aggressively supportive."[67] This puts great pressure on CEOs and heads of HR, but since this is such a profound barrier, it must be addressed and swiftly remedied.

Another barrier I often encounter is lack of expertise. Many

66 Stephen Drotter and John Prescott, *The Succession Pipeline: How to Get the Talent You Need When You Need It* (Carlsbad: Motivational Press, 2018), 95.

67 Stephen Drotter and John Prescott, *The Succession Pipeline: How to Get the Talent You Need When You Need It* (Carlsbad: Motivational Press, 2018), 96.

senior leaders and HR personnel don't know the components of a plan or how to rally their people around it. As previously discussed, leaders need to remain vulnerable and admit their own blind spots. If you're a senior leader or HR person, now is the time to discover the strategic plan and people plan for your organization. Your organization's performance and viability is at stake.

A SAMPLE TEMPLATE FOR STRATEGIC PLANNING:

Purpose and Outcomes:

- Review and agree on purpose of strategic planning and what success looks like.
- Discuss/develop/refine and document the Vision.
- Discuss/develop/refine and document the Mission.
- Discuss/develop/refine and document the Values.

Vision:

- Define where organization wants to be in three to five years.
- What is the future state of affairs?
- Make it tangible so that we know when the vision has been achieved.

Mission:

- Define what the organization does today.
- How do others see the organization?
- Ensure that this statement is the template for making

decisions about what we do on a daily basis.

Values:

- What do we believe our decisions and behaviors are based on? What do we live and breathe by?

- How do we ensure these values are communicated and demonstrated throughout the company?

- Is there a way we can relate these values to the "Core Values" statement we publish for those outside the company?

- Give examples of how these values are operationalized and ensured on a regular basis.

Another common response I hear is that senior leaders don't have the time or the budget to devote to developing a people plan. As we've discussed, however, strategy alignment is a key indicator for business performance. When viewed in this way, it's not a valid excuse to say you don't have the time and money to invest in your organization's success.

Another barrier is that some senior leaders and/or HR staff feel like their strategies change so frequently that it's unrealistic to develop people strategies as well. When strategies change frequently, however, that's more reason to have a people plan in place to bolster the organization amid a disruptive environment.

As organizational development researchers noted in the *Harvard Business Review*, organizations are "systems of interacting elements: Roles, responsibilities, and relationships are defined by organizational structure, processes, leadership styles, people's professional and cultural backgrounds, and HR policies and practices. And it doesn't recognize that all those elements together drive organizational behavior and performance. If the system does not change, it will not support and sustain individual behavior change—indeed, it will set people up to fail."[68] Organizations are inherently chaotic, and they need to be in order to drive "behavior and performance." Using the disruptive environment as a barrier to development, rather than a reason for it, is shortsighted, and as these researchers note, it sets employees up for failure.

Another barrier to connecting the people plan and strategic plan is HR not being valued. When this happens, there may be a blatant omission of people strategies, or in some cases, senior leaders never thought to create a plan for the people in the first place. As we've said before, leaders don't know what they don't know. This again puts a great amount of pressure on HR leaders, but with their role comes great responsibility. A strong HR team is a factor in an organization's viability and must have a strong voice at the table. They must be the experts who guide the rest of the leadership team

Not every HR leader is up to the task, nor is every CEO. The reality, however, is that if you are not up for the challenge of leadership, and if you lack the courage to enact systemic change, then you have already failed your leaders. Joining the leadership development revolution takes a tremendous amount of bravery. When leaders can muster it *for their people*, the people see and feel engaged and motivated to align with the greater organizational strategies.

Understanding the direct link between strategy alignment and business success allows for transformational change within an organization. In order to be successful, executives *must* connect leadership

---

68 Michael Beer, Magnus Finnström, and Derek Schrader, "Why Leadership Training Fails—And What to Do About It," *Harvard Business Review*, October 2016, https://hbr.org/2016/10/why-leadership-training-fails-and-what-to-do-about-it.

strategy with business strategy. There are no excuses. When strategies are aligned, organizations show proven results in performance and sustainability. With continually shifting markets and technologies, the need for strategy alignment is more important than ever.

MIKE SHAVER, CEO OF CHILDREN'S HOME & AID, ON LEADERSHIP:

We're in the process of beginning to undergo a strategic planning process. One of the things that we have talked about is that between any good strategy and operational excellence—which is what you want at the end of that process—sits organizational culture, and how the organization reinforces what it takes to live that strategy and advance that strategy on a regular basis. It doesn't do that if it just sits on a poster. Even if you blow it up and you frame it, that isn't what does it. What does it is when you can give everybody a sense of the direction that the organization is going and what that work means for them.

It's about the *why* behind what it is that you're trying to accomplish, the aspirational idea that aligns people and gets them to see that the strategy is about producing a different kind of impact. Then you cultivate that in your execution and the way you set expectations for leaders to push that down in the organization.

If you haven't prepared, and you haven't developed that leadership competency within the people who have those responsibilities across the organization, their ability to articulate and tackle the more aspirational ideas around what you are trying to achieve as an organization is really limited. They will find themselves trapped in the tactical.

The importance and the value of leadership development across the organization is really about ensuring that there's the ability for everybody in the organization to see how they are an active participant in leading this effort, and being part of the work that we're trying to channel. The traditional model does not connect more broadly to the organization. Not only is that a mistake, it's also a missed opportunity to enlist a lot of capable, talented, bright people into lifting up and ensuring that your strategy does lead to operational excellence.

CHAPTER 6

Follow the Leader

One of the reasons leadership development is difficult to discuss, much less agree upon, is because of its intangibility. The definition of a strong leader is inherently abstract, making it tricky to pin down the endgame exactly. It gets murkier still when we talk about the components of leader-led development and what makes it successful. In order for development to be fruitful, top leadership must drive the people plan. Effective development, however, doesn't stop there.

There is a people component and a functional component to any leader's job. For example, a leader in customer service is responsible for service and volume metrics, whereas a leader in manufacturing is responsible for high-quality products. In addition, both of these leaders are tasked with maintaining little turnover, engagement of their teams, and developing people to execute more valuable tasks over time.

A leader is in a unique position to know where each direct report should focus, to see them in action, and to know their progress. This is why leaders are so valuable—because they know the company, the people, and the situations and are able to guide others in the right direction. Ideally, this perspective allows leaders to know what is next for their direct reports and offers them opportunities to provide resources to help direct reports get there.

Furthermore, leaders offer daily support—through coaching—to employees in their growth and their skill set for the role that they're playing, as well as helping them identify and transition to future roles. Leaders who know their direct reports' strengths and weaknesses are better positioned to distribute work and determine development needs in response to the observed gaps. In truth, we all need varying degrees of development throughout our careers. For example, one of Oliver Group's highly tenured employees continually excelled in most areas but needed technology support. It is his leader's job to know his future goals in leveraging technology, assess his current state, and identify how to get him the technology learning he needs. Without it, he may not continue advancing in his role.

In short, a leader's job is to identify an employee's future goals, determine what and how they're doing today, establish the gap between the two, and provide resources and support to close that gap. Direct reports might need assignments on some special projects—for example, to adopt a new skillset or to transform a behavior that is a barrier to advancement.

A leader's job is to identify an employee's future goals, determine what and how they're doing today, establish the gap between the two, and provide resources and support to close that gap.

A leader's primary role is to coach. This daily internal development can oftentimes alleviate the need for formal development. Daily coaching means finding opportunities to converse with individuals about intended goals, understanding the current situation and opportunities and options that exist therein, and then determining actions to take. They must lead the development plan, support direct reports through it daily, and then provide extra resources as needed. When a leader can't necessarily assist in every scenario, however, or needs external resources, they might turn to external coaches to help direct reports advance to the next level.

External coaching is an aspect of development that can overlap or augment leadership's daily coaching. Private coaching is a one-on-one exchange of thinking and information between two people to work on specific developmental pieces to reach their goals. Typically, external coaches spend four to six hours per month working on an individual's specific opportunity or challenge.

WHEN DOES A LEADER NEED AN OUTSIDE COACH?

- When managing through a transition/new job or when new skills or tasks need to be adopted quickly

- To shore up an important behavior or skill to do their job more effectively with time compression or because of complexity of the work

- When added resources would help a high-potential leader move faster to hit his/her goals

- To handle business and personal challenges where confidentiality is paramount to the outcome

- When a leader of the individual isn't skilled in developing certain competencies

For example, a sales leader, Rebecca, requested a budget for outside coaching for one of her direct reports. She had been trying to help David overcome relationship challenges he was experiencing with his peers. Rebecca had coached him on a daily basis to curb his aggression and "neediness," as described by the account management team. Rebecca didn't think she had more time to spend with David and had exhausted all of her ideas. However, because she knew him and his motives well, she believed he wanted to work on the relationships, and she understood that he would be more successful if he could overcome this challenge.

Rebecca decided to bring in an outside coach who assessed the situation and agreed to help him with his internal relationships. The coach and David created strategies and new methods and talked regularly about progress and next steps. In the end, Rebecca couldn't help David improve, but she recognized his need and sought him the resources he required. Over a six-month period, David was able to turn the relationships around. Soon, his peers were seeking him out instead of avoiding him. He was thankful for the support and increased his sales by 25 percent the following year. It was a win-win!

EXTERNAL COACHING BENEFITS:

- Not constrained by politics—can remain unbiased
- Accredited in coaching and knows techniques and approaches for each learning opportunity
- Confidentiality as someone outside of the company
- Can find a specific coach for each leader or situation
- Coach invested in an individual, not a company
- If coaching many, can identify themes among leaders coached and create a broader solution to problems

Leaders are responsible for the outcome, but they can't force someone to change. As a leader who practices daily coaching, rather than direct people, you assist them in coming to their own conclusions and reaching their own place of understanding. Coaches do this by having the coachee determine what they need help with in order to reach their goals. Using an individual-led approach, coaching is about giving coachees some added knowledge or new ways of thinking. Like Rebecca, they are the direct report's ally and confidante and give a boost to performance.

THE VALUE OF LEADER-LED ENVIRONMENT

Though it may vary by role, generally the value of a leader is in preparing people for the future, supporting direct reports, and helping the overall organization succeed. When direct reports work in a leader-led environment, they feel supported, validated, and valued, which leads to deeper engagement and higher performance. As we've discussed, engagement is a retention strategy because employees who are engaged in the goals and progress of an organization and who see the potential to advance within it are more likely to stay.

Effective leaders can be powerful motivators. Employees want to know they are part of something big and not just a cog in the machine. They want to know how they can add value, that their role contributes to the overall success of the organization. Purpose needs to be part of a leader's approach, both in their own work and in how they cultivate their direct reports. Authors of *The Succession Pipeline* assert that the leader "sets the tone for the whole organization. The organization's top management is sensitive to the seriousness of purpose that the CEO displays. If the CEO is dedicated, everyone else will likely follow his or her lead."[69] When a leader imbues "the seriousness of purpose," and uses it to drive development, direct reports feel supported and validated.

Employees need to feel that the organization trusts them and sees their potential. This means that they need to see future roles available to them. In order to do this, leaders must be developed by levels. Leaders provide different value based on whether they are leading individual contributors, other leaders, leaders of leaders, or a function. A leader is not just a leader, as every level requires different performance expectations and value contributions to the organization. For each level, there is unique work to value, time to allocate, and skills to apply.

LEVELS OF LEADERSHIP:

Leader of Self: This is an individual who is responsible for their work and no one else's. They must focus on prioritizing their work and completing quality tasks on time. They have to be a team player and accept the company's values.

Leader of Others: This leader manages individual contributors, and the leader's success is defined by their direct reports' success. They are responsible for the work of other people and the collective efforts of the team. They focus on selecting individuals and building the team and performance management. Communication is a key skill at this level.

Leader of Leaders: These leaders are responsible for other leaders and must be more comfortable navigating relationships. They focus on selecting leaders and building the organization's capability, managing boundaries, and allocating

---

69   Stephen Drotter and John Prescott, *The Succession Pipeline: How to Get the Talent You Need When You Need It* (Carlsbad: Motivational Press, 2018), 257.

resources for their area. Overall, they are responsible for the climate of their area, as they influence other leaders.

Functional Leaders: These are leaders responsible for a function of the business and building a functional competitive advantage. For example, they could lead finance, HR, IT, or other functions of a business. At this level they need to be a full member of the leadership/business unit team while driving functional excellence. They are also owners of developing leadership talent throughout the organization.

Business Leaders: Business leaders are at the top of an organization and select functional leaders and lead with a multifunctional perspective while developing and executing the business strategy.

Each level has unique responsibilities and requirements. By understanding levels of leadership, each leader can understand their purpose, the overall execution of the business plan, what work they should value, and where they should spend their time.

LEVELS OF LEADERSHIP

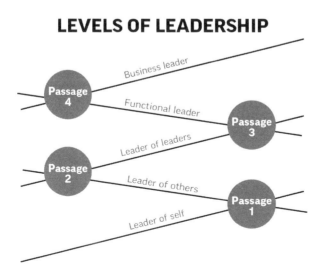

One level must be mastered before moving to the next level for optimal success. Moving into a new leadership level requires letting go of old responsibilities and assuming new ones. There are skills you need at every transition, along with a change in the work you value and where you spend your time. Even if you fit a role behaviorally and cognitively, you still need other competencies based on level of leadership. Not only does this allow employees to understand their current role and potential future roles, but it also ensures that organizations are looking at succession and promotion from within.

COMPONENTS OF A LEADER-LED ENVIRONMENT

Everyone has a story about a leader who was terrible. We might not know what that leader was lacking, but we know a bad leader when we're led by one. Despite the ambiguities, we can all discern a bad leadership environment versus a good one when we see it, but it's much more complicated to distinguish *why* one is better than the other. How do you distinguish if an environment is leader-led? How do you know if a leader is driving the process?

Effective leaders understand the components of a leader-led environment. They appreciate the importance of building good direct report relationships and how to tie their individual values into their leadership values. They often employ a style that helps engage their direct reports and make them feel taken care of. Leader-led environments teach other leaders within their organization how to do their jobs using proven methods of human learning and build a culture that values development. Lastly, they foster a leadership mindset that helps them lead the organization toward success.

A Leader-Led Environment Fosters Relationships

A leader's job is never "finished." Leaders are building for the future, which requires them to build relationships and connections. Furthermore, they cultivate relationships built on trust so that their feedback is welcomed and integrated. When leaders invest in connection, their direct reports know their leader has their back. People only want to learn from those they trust and value. Effective leadership must also include selflessness because sometimes a leader may be good at developing people, only to lose them when they take their acquired skills somewhere else. With a leader-led approach, it's okay to lose some direct reports whose development qualifies them for another opportunity. This means that the leader's priorities are in order and they are truly invested in the growth of their people.

A Leader-Led Environment Values a Culture of Learning

Ideally a leader understands that their work benefits the entire organization. In *Sustaining Change: Leadership That Works*, authors Deborah Rowland and Malcom Higgs acknowledge that leaders need to let go of their own professional success and instead focus on organizational success: "[A leader's] task is to build their capability of the organizational system (i.e. talent, structure, energy, innovation processes) to generate the performance outcomes rather than directly control the performance outcomes themselves."[70] There is no room for personal ego in the development of leaders.

A good example of how an effective leader uses his own success to inspire others can be seen in our work with Michael Foreman, CEO of FS Investments. He explained to me that he wanted to transfer what he learned over the years to people who are starting out in hopes of mitigating their challenges and expediting their successes. During regular town halls with leaders, he shared his own lessons on what led to his success—including discussions about discipline, mental focus, health habits (exercise, food, and sleep), giving back,

---

70 Deborah Rowland and Malcolm Higgs, *Sustaining Change: Leadership That Works* (San Francisco: Josey-Bass, 2008), 94.

and maintaining self-awareness and determination. He shared these lessons in an effort to build a culture of learning, which is essential for developing and valuing leaders. He is a prime example of how leader-led initiatives prioritize people development and value a culture that promotes learning and development.

Leaders who intentionally build a culture of learning place much value on the individual, which is at odds with standard development practices. According to Corporate Executive Board research of fifteen hundred senior managers at fifty organizations, three-quarters of them were unhappy with their companies' learning and development, but only one in four felt it was critical to their business outcomes.[71] When you look at numbers like these, it is easy to see why the standard development isn't working: because it's not valued. So much of learning and development success depends on the culture in which it is created and implemented. This responsibility falls to the leader. They must lead the development and foster the valuing of it across the organization.

> *Leaders who intentionally build a culture of learning place much value on the individual, which is at odds with standard development practices.*

Research by Amy Edmonson of Harvard Business School and Anita Woolley of Carnegie Mellon compared the outcomes of corporate development programs that aimed to improve problem-solving and communication between leaders and their direct reports. Though the programs were the same, they discovered that success varied across the company depending on the previously established

---

71   Michael Beer, Magnus Finnström, and Derek Schrader, "Why Leadership Training Fails—And What to Do About It," *Harvard Business Review*, October 2016, https://hbr.org/2016/10/why-leadership-training-fails-and-what-to-do-about-it.

culture. Those companies that showed the greatest improvements were the ones that had already developed a "psychologically safe" environment where employees felt free to speak up.[72] This is why building a culture that values people development is so vital to its success. Development is more likely to effect real change in organizations that have cultivated a climate where development interventions can blossom.

A Leader-Led Environment Distinguishes between Individual Values versus Leadership Values

Leaders use their own values and ethics to "inspire people," but not as a replacement for daily leadership. There is a difference between a personal value and a leadership value. For example, a leader might value candor, but the applicable leadership value is to value coaching on a daily basis. You must also honor your leaders and show them through their own development. As a leader of leaders or a leader of others, you are not an island. You must find ways to connect to your people and the larger organizational strategies.

An effective leader also understands that the key to development "sticking" is understanding what their direct reports are trying to accomplish. If they don't recognize that, they can't help them get there. Research shows that education and development gain the most traction when efforts are championed by senior leaders who can "motivate people to learn and change; create the conditions for them to apply what they've studied; foster immediate improvements in individual and organizational effectiveness; and put in place systems

---

72 Amy C. Edmondson and Anita W. Wooley, "Understanding Outcomes of Organizational Learning Interventions," in *Blackwell Handbook of Organizational Learning and Knowledge Management*, eds. M. Easterby-Smith and M. Lyles (Malden: Blackwell Publishing, 2003).

that help sustain the learning."[73]

This is when creating a development plan for each direct report—and *with* each direct report—is so vital to the leader-led environment. Furthermore, the reports should be measured regularly against the plan. This is how you build a true, valued culture of learning. If leaders and direct reports both agree on what needs developed and how to get the skills, knowledge, and abilities, then leaders can coach direct reports daily to help them achieve those goals, leveraging their personal and leadership values.

A Leader-Led Environment Drives Development

In his book *Neuropsychology for Coaches*, organizational psychologist Dr. Paul Brown calls the leader-led approach to development "effective coaching"—though it also applies to leadership development—which he defines as:[74]

> the capacity … to so understand and manage the brain processes of the person who is being coached that effective change and development within that person, plus the consideration of change and development, is deliberately created and consolidated for that person's benefit, bounded by what has been agreed contractually between the two people involved.

Once a leader understands the gap between current and future state of a direct report, they can determine if this person is or will be a fit for the future needs of the business. The leader has a unique view and obligation to fit these two pieces together. I've said it before

---

73 Michael Beer, Magnus Finnström, and Derek Schrader, "Why Leadership Training Fails—And What to Do About It," *Harvard Business Review*, October 2016, https://hbr.org/2016/10/why-leadership-training-fails-and-what-to-do-about-it.

74 Paul Brown and Virginia Brown, *Neuropsychology for Coaches* (New York: Open University Press, 2012), 5.

and I'll say it again: the leader has to guide the development. The leader can bring in a coach to further support the individual, but that doesn't at all take away the leader's daily job. Leaders must lead the development and be actively involved at all stages, at all times.

A Leader-Led Environment Honors Adult Learning

Though it sounds obvious, a good leader must have a keen understanding of adult human learning. As we discussed in chapter 2, one of the reasons smile sheet assessments were ineffective was because they only reflected what a cohort was exposed to in development, not what they retained. True retention of new knowledge is seen in changed behavior. How do we change behavior? By using proven teaching strategies that can effect true change.

Neuroscience has revealed that humans learn best when emotional brain circuits are activated. This is why the traditional lecture-based learning fails. Learners need dynamic, experiential, visceral learning environments in order to activate emotional circuits in the brain and have the best chance of affecting behavior. Deborah Rowland notes that, "If leadership development begins in the head, leaders will stay in their heads. We can't simply think our way out of a habit. But in experience, and novel experience in particular, our intentional mind can be more engaged as we make conscious decisions about our behavior."[75] It is a leader's job to create these "novel experiences" that can enact true change.

There is a way to help someone get from point A to point B without explicitly telling them. These subtle distinctions in leadership style and delivery are everything when it comes to successful outcomes and behavioral change. Rowland and Higgs distinguish

---

75   Deborah Rowland, "Why Leadership Development Isn't Developing Leaders," *Harvard Business Review*, October 14, 2016, https://hbr.org/2016/10/why-leadership-development-isnt-developing-leaders.

between what they call "framing" versus "shaping" leadership styles. Framing leaders provide context and support for their direct reports, whereas shaping leaders promote leader-centric directives. Their research has statistically proven that framing leaders are more successful in implementing larger, more complex changes: "They work *with* the organization to help people see why change is necessary, they establish a firm overall direction, a set of guiding principles, and a high-level sense of agenda and journey for the change process, and then leave space for people to get on with it."[76] Space to grow and be? Now *that* sounds like leader-led development.

On the contrary, they concluded a shaping leader was not able to implement organizational changes effectively: "This style, which is very leader-centric, tends to either create dependency in the organization on the individual leader or indeed create factions who want to resist the leader."[77] Can you see why the subtle distinction can create a lot of headaches for senior leaders? Though this leadership style may have been popular generations ago, it has been proven ineffective. It harms all people across the organization and the organization itself. Furthermore, it bogs down leaders and inhibits them from leading at their level.

It's hard to know what someone *should* do but refrain from telling them (ask any parent!). Yet a successful leader gets someone to the place where change is welcomed and supported. They've created a culture conducive to change, and then they step back and let the individual enact the change. That is the only way true change happens. Change will happen because the individual sees the need for it and is motivated and inspired to do it. The person also needs

---

76 Deborah Rowland and Malcolm Higgs, *Sustaining Change: Leadership That Works* (San Francisco: Josey-Bass, 2008), 93.

77 Deborah Rowland and Malcolm Higgs, *Sustaining Change: Leadership That Works* (San Francisco: Josey-Bass, 2008), 93.

to understand the benefit of the change, and this is why leaders need to tie development into evaluations or other incentivized measures.

Good leadership development takes development from the classroom to the office. Lessons are most impactful when leaders get on-the-spot feedback that is directly connected to their work. This feedback and other evaluative measures that compare against the original development plan—making sure it's connected back to the strategic plan—are crucial for adult learning to "stick."

Employees can drive their own learning along with their bosses. After they've had the foundational pieces in place, they can continue to identify their specific development needs and work with their supervisors to meet them. Not everyone has the same needs. After you've got the foundational pieces of a job, you might still require skills like technical support, financial understanding, executive presence, or strategic thinking. When learning is leader-led, leaders can help determine exactly what their direct reports need to drive their learning and meet their full potential.

A Leader-Led Environment Fosters a Development Mindset

An effective leader has rewired their own thinking and adopted a leadership mindset that promotes growth and development. In 2008, Google embarked on a multiyear internal study called Project Oxygen that analyzed more than ten thousand observations of its managers to determine the eight habits of its most effective leaders. They found that the most important attribute was a leader's mindset. Remember when I said at the opening of the chapter that leadership development is hard to discuss because of its intangibility? Well, talking about a leadership mindset can also be hazy, even for those of us in the space. So what is this mindset, and more importantly, how can you implement it for your own—and your team's—leadership success?

One's mindset, though an opaque concept, determines their worldview. It informs how they behave, react, process, and develop. Dr. Carol Dweck, professor of psychology at Stanford University, calls it "the view you adopt of yourself" that "can determine whether you accomplish the things you value."[78]

The crux of a development mindset means focusing less on doing the work and more on developing others to do the work. The shift requires a leader to realize the value they add through their leadership role, and thus, focus on their primary job to lead and develop the team. For Rowland and Higgs, the key to unlocking effective leadership is through this subtle shift in awareness. This awareness "brings increased insight which generates choice and ability to respond differently."[79] They assert that effective leaders use this mindset in more "mindful and creative ways."[80] Once the leader is engaged—or leading the development—the organizational system transforms.

Leaders don't get a free pass. The buck stops with you. As Dweck asserts, you must have the right mindset to maximize your leadership potential and capitalize on your organization's strengths and your people's development. It's not enough, however, to stop with an established leadership mindset; you must then let that mindset inform your daily interactions and decision-making.

One study from Rowland and Higgs found that a leader's "theoretical understanding" about changing their leadership mindset didn't bear on their success in doing so.[81] They observed

---

78 Carol Dweck, *Mindset: The New Psychology of Success* (New York: Ballantine Books, 2007), 6.

79 Deborah Rowland and Malcolm Higgs, *Sustaining Change: Leadership That Works* (San Francisco: Josey-Bass, 2008), 360.

80 Ibid.

81 Deborah Rowland and Malcolm Higgs, *Sustaining Change: Leadership That Works* (San Francisco: Josey-Bass, 2008), 96.

that the more a leader advanced through senior leadership, the more attention they paid to "the quality of their thinking and the rigor of their planning—not to the quality of their behavior and what they do."[82] They explained that though planning and thinking are indeed important for leaders, "leaders should pay equal attention to *how* they go about their work—how they engage with others, how they set up meetings, how they have conversations, how they create meaning in the organization."[83]

Leader developers can't possibly train everyone in everything they need from a programmatic approach. For this reason, leaders need to help their direct reports learn on a daily basis. This requires a shift to the leadership mindset that calls on leaders to always be in the mode of learning, without stopping. Leaders must get in the habit of asking a lot of questions about their team's work and talents and make sure that annual performance reviews and goal setting happens and is reviewed regularly.

A development mindset is not a secret formula. It's a discipline that should be cultivated and practiced daily. In order to create robust and dynamic organizations that have dedicated and engaged workers, the leader must be ready to assume a development mindset that allows for growth and development at all levels of leadership. This is how leaders can rewire their minds and transform their teams.

THE BARRIERS TO LEADER-LED DEVELOPMENT

If senior leaders understand the value of effective leadership and understand how to get there, why aren't they doing it? Because some of the barriers seem insurmountable. In some cases, creating leader-led development might require some systemic changes, but those are

---

82   Ibid.

83   Ibid.

worth it to have engaged and committed employees dedicated to the organization's mission.

WHAT GETS IN THE WAY OF LEADER-LED DEVELOPMENT?

- Faulty policies and practices
- Time
- Don't know how to develop people
- Don't see the value
- Lack of accountability

One of the larger barriers to effective development are faulty policies and procedures. This is, of course, not a quick fix. Though senior leaders don't often want to accept the uncomfortable reality that their policies and procedures are broken, it is often the key to unlocking their organization's full potential. If it's broken, you must fix it.

When it comes to failing development programs, professor and author Michael Beer points the finger at senior leaders and HR managers. He asserts that the problem doesn't lie in "individuals' deficiencies but, rather, in the policies and practices created by top management. *Those* are the things to fix before training can succeed longer-term. It's much easier for HR to point to employees' competencies as the problem and to training as the clear solution. That's a message senior leaders are receptive to hearing."[84]

---

84 Michael Beer, Magnus Finnström, and Derek Schrader, "Why Leadership Training Fails—And What to Do About It," *Harvard Business Review*, October 2016, https://hbr.org/2016/10/why-leadership-training-fails-and-what-to-do-about-it.

ARE YOUR POLICIES AND PROCEDURES BARRIERS TO LEADER-LED DEVELOPMENT?

- Do you reward your leaders on their team members' readiness for the next role?

- Do your leaders have a review where discussions of impact include the preparation of their direct reports?

- Do leaders have an active voice in whether their direct reports are considered for other roles in different parts of the organization?

Another barrier to creating a leader-led culture is time. Almost daily, I hear senior leaders claim they have no time to develop their people. It feels like a burden to have performance discussions or end-of-year reviews. My advice is simple: your main job is to develop other people—that's why you're called a leader. If you want the job, you must do the job. These leaders often feel that the daily leadership responsibilities get in the way of their functional output. It's true that senior leaders need to do both. They must value the leadership role and find time to commit to it. It must be something they recognize and seek to revolutionize themselves.

> *My advice is simple: your main job is to develop other people—that's why you're called a leader. If you want the job, you must do the job.*

Even when leaders find the time, however, they might not know how to develop other people. If this is the case, the leader must seek outside help in the form of external organizational development professionals. Furthermore, leaders might not see the value of development. There is copious research that shows investing in development offers measurable results. The research in this book should give all leaders a clear understanding of the link between the two. As leadership strategist Josh Bersin succinctly states, "A company's level of maturity in their leadership development has a greater impact on their long-term business performance than almost all else."[85] If leaders don't see it as their job—because it's not tied to compensation or there's a lack of accountability—there need to be some larger adjustments in policies and procedures so that people, and their development, are valued and rewarded. Though these barriers require time and effort to overcome, development is the surest way to bolster your teams and organizations.

I recognize it's not easy to make some of these larger systemic changes. But doing nothing almost guarantees your organization's demise. According to the World Economic Forum's *The Future of Jobs Report*, as industries change and evolve, by 2022, at least 54 percent of all employees will require significant "upskilling" or training.[86] If leaders don't adapt their thinking and shore up their development programs now, they will experience unprecedented disruptions in the future.

Effective leaders also understand that the autocratic leadership style of the past has no room in today's practice. Authors and researchers Rowland and Higgs recognize: [87]

[T]he charismatic heroic leader does not necessarily create

---

85   Josh Bersin, "It's Not The CEO, It's The Leadership Strategy That Matters," *Forbes*, July 30, 2012. https://www.forbes.com/sites/joshbersin/2012/07/30/its-not-the-ceo-its-the-leadership-strategy-that-matters/#2cc65ace6db8.

86   World Economic Forum, "The Future of Jobs Report 2018," http://www3.weforum.org/docs/WEF_Future_of_Jobs_2018.pdf.

87   Deborah Rowland and Malcolm Higgs, *Sustaining Change: Leadership That Works* (San Francisco: Josey-Bass, 2008), 93.

sustained greatness in an organisation. Rather, the more humble, modest, and enabling leaders are better placed to create an organisation that day by day moves … towards its future. These kinds of leaders give others the freedom and space to excel, though within a highly disciplined framework. They inspire people through standards of excellence rather than charisma. They seek power through people and not over people.

The alarm is sounding, and it has been for decades. The current development plans aren't working, and our organizations and teams are suffering as a result. It's time to say goodbye to the heroic leader of the past who lets barriers remain in her path, and to embrace the revolutionary leader who prioritizes development and has the courage to lead the way. Now is the time to act. Leaders must lead their teams toward a future that—despite its myriad of disruptions—has opportunities for growth, engagement, and purpose.

MICHAEL FOREMAN, CEO OF FS INVESTMENTS, ON LEADERSHIP:

Like my team of leaders, I became a better leader through early experiences I had at FS Investments. As we accrued more corporate and managerial experience and became more self-aware, we became stronger leaders of a more successful company. We went from a gritty, rough-and-tumble start-up to a larger, more sophisticated financial company.

One specific lesson I learned from my mentor at Oliver Group was to focus on building trust. Before that, I had never thought about trust. I now tell my leaders to find someone—family, colleagues, professors, bosses—they can talk to who really understands them. Inventory those close to you, and ask for their help.

To build trust with my direct reports, we have regular forums that are honest and direct. All are encouraged to ask questions and provide feedback because I believe leaders need to adapt their style for their people. For this reason, I try and be objective and adjust based on what is needed from my direct reports.

It is my responsibility—shared with my HR leader—to develop our people. Our people plan is separate from our strategic plan, though our HR leader sits on the committee that drafts the strategic plan to ensure alignment. We also stack rank our people and use 360-degree feedback to create measurable ways to assess our leaders.

I do wish that as a young leader, I had focused more on building trust with my team. This has been a great lesson for me. I'd also want to know that I could slow down and everything would be okay; I'd still be successful. With time, I've learned that I don't need to be the smartest person in the room, which comes back to having self-awareness and being patient with how things play out.

CHAPTER 7

Practice Makes Progress

One recent client was a real estate investment trust company that experienced rapid growth in a short amount of time. Their growth was so exponential, in fact, that it began to create leadership development challenges. They had a lot of new leaders within the company, and many were early in their tenure. There wasn't a lot of day-to-day development happening through leadership. When they contacted us about developing over one hundred leaders from their total of five hundred employees, the senior leaders were so taxed for time that they opted not to be involved in the development process. Despite their recognition that development was needed, they were not connected to the people development, much less driving it.

Without the senior team's involvement, we devised and delivered development programs. According to the feedback scores attained after the programs, all went well. The leaders had retained the information they received all four days, and they were motivated to act on their new learning. We encouraged the company to engage in follow-up coaching to ensure the learning was properly integrated, but the senior team didn't want to spend additional dollars. After trying to help HR convince the leadership team, it seemed that we had done all that we could. The rest was up to the organization's leaders to make sure their development efforts weren't wasted.

Not long after the programs, their HR team shared their concerns that the leaders weren't changing as much as they had hoped. They were right—some of the development couldn't stick because it wasn't reinforced by their supervisors, the senior team, or by coaches. They didn't have time, and they didn't know the content in order to reinforce it because they hadn't participated. Despite our suggestions, they failed to deliver the Third Driver of Leader Development Success: *Leaders must be able to put into play the skills they learn.*

Leaders attended the programs, but they weren't able to put what they had learned into practice because senior leadership wasn't reinforcing it. It wasn't the cohorts' fault. Instead, they returned to work—to the innately chaotic, frenetic nature of their industry—and the pace was too fast. Leaders of the program participants didn't free them up and didn't reinforce the concepts, so cohorts couldn't take the time to practice the material. As a result, the learning was somewhat lost.

Though my team felt optimistic about the programs and the delivery, those variables are not enough to drive successful outcomes. Having the supervisors understand the expectations of the programs and tie those to their own expectations would have allowed for better outcomes. When this happens, cohorts are encouraged and motivated to practice their learning. The more they *experience* the learning, the more it "sticks" and results in the changed behavior we seek.

For my team, there has been a good deal of learning through

client interactions such as these. Moving forward, we no longer work with organizations that won't incorporate the Four Drivers of Leader Development Success, because as mentioned, doing *some* of them doesn't garner success. Though we can make suggestions for other reinforcements, if the organization opts out—as it did in this example—there is little we can do.

The company ended up with one hundred people with leadership knowledge, which was helpful but not the outcome we desired. We weren't sure how their development impacted the company directly. Though the organization benefited in the sense that these leaders had a better understanding of their roles and were thus better leaders as a result, the company opted not to measure the business impact. Oliver Group did measure their knowledge and behavior change, and found the cohorts' scores remained high six months later, but they were not putting into practice what they had learned. As a result, we knew there wouldn't be sustained behavioral change in the future.

This organization was so close to getting it right—in fact, they could have turned it around if the senior team drove a few changes in how they rewarded and set expectations for their leaders. They needed to provide leaders with supportive resources for questions, follow-up, and reinforcement. Unfortunately, as their adviser, we couldn't coerce them to do these things, and therefore, overall benefits were limited.

This example shows the reality of being an adviser and not having control of all the outcomes. We can always make suggestions, but that doesn't ensure they are integrated. Because this organization didn't incorporate the Four Drivers of Leader Development Success, the learning didn't stick like it could have and should have. People within the leadership industry have to become more comfortable talking about scenarios that *didn't* work so that we can learn from them and help other clients go in with eyes wide open. We can give an organization the tools, but we can't pressure them to use them or reinforce them.

Let this be your cautionary tale: you can spend thousands of dollars and hours on leadership development, but if the knowledge is not applied, then there will not be systemic change. For this company, they weren't using the learning because senior leaders didn't drive it and reinforcement it afterward. Other companies we work with provide the direction and reinforcement, and they enjoy systemic benefits at all levels and have leaders ready for whatever comes their way. Let's look closer at the ways organizations can reinforce the learning they offer and how they can profit from people development.

WHAT DOES REINFORCEMENT LOOK LIKE?

As we've discussed, learning isn't successful unless it creates changed behavior. All the development in the world won't do cohorts any good if leaders don't see changes in how they perform their duties. This requires participants' leaders to actively reinforce and support their direct reports after development. In fact, when the development programs are done, that's when senior leaders' work begins.

1. Learning Requires Immediacy of Application

Development cannot work unless it is customized to teach adults how they learn best. There are many ways in which adult learning (andragogy) differs from child learning (pedagogy). According to adult educator Malcolm Knowles, andragogy is comprised of four crucial assumptions that differ from the assumptions about child learners: self-concept, experience, readiness to learn, orientation to learning, and motivation to learn. It's Knowles's "orientation to learning" that speaks to the Third Driver of Leader Development Success. Knowles concluded that in order for adults to integrate new information, it must connect back to their prior experiences and be immediately applied.

This opportunity exists when cohorts return to their day-to-day jobs after formal programs. It doesn't matter how large the development initiative is at an organization; development only makes a difference if leaders have the opportunity to incorporate what they've learned into their daily work. Without reinforcement, learning is lost, and development is blocked.

2. Learning Must Connect to the Real World

We know from decades of research that Knowles's early principles about adult learning have remained relevant. Neuroscience further supports Knowles's assumptions by showing that learning is best retained (and later shows up through changed behavior) when emotional brain circuits are activated. How do we do that? Through experiences. Author Deborah Rowland asserts:[88]

> Visceral, lived experiences best activate [emotional brain] circuits; they prompt us to notice both things in the environment and what's going on inside ourselves. If leadership development begins in the head, leaders will stay in their heads. We can't simply think our way out of a habit. But in experience, and novel experience in particular, our intentional mind can be more engaged as we make conscious decisions about our behavior.

In order to activate emotional circuits and create sustainable behavior change, learning must connect to the leader's real world. If a leader of others attends four days of development, for example,

---

88   Deborah Rowland, "Why Leadership Development Isn't Developing Leaders," *Harvard Business Review*, October 14, 2016, https://hbr.org/2016/10/why-leadership-development-isnt-developing-leaders.

they are surrounded by their peers and all of their varied perspectives. This environment encourages a mindset shift that allows them to realize the value of their work, how to do it more adeptly, and how to spend their time effectively. These methods of interaction connect the concepts to the real world.

Once they return to their day-to-day environment, however, they might wonder how to make their time away count. If, for example, they have weekly meetings with their direct reports, what are they going to do differently in those meetings? How are they going to coach a direct report versus directing a direct report? How are they going to talk about performance more often than once a year? How are they going to make sure that each of their direct reports understands his/her part of the strategy?

The solution is having a development plan by the end of each program. After cohorts learn from each other and the facilitator, they need to devise a plan moving forward. They connect what they have learned to their real working world through a plan of action that considers how they will incorporate new ways of thinking and doing. This plan is created at the end of each module through exercises with their own direct reports in mind. They need to ask, *What am I going to do when I get back to my job to make sure that this gets done and that it is reinforced?* They need to know who they might seek support from to make this work. Learning won't stick unless they leave the training room understanding how to put the learning into play in their real world.

As we've discussed, learning can be a bit hazy and abstract. For this reason, incorporating learning into a person's job description or performance goals is another powerful way to reinforce behavior. When this happens, all parties understand exactly what is expected of them, and they are incentivized to be creative and incorporate their development daily.

3. Learning Must Be Supported by Senior Leaders

Senior leaders have to connect development to their strategy. They must also cultivate a culture where development is encouraged and where leaders have an obligation to develop their people as the *priority* of their job. Senior leaders and leaders of others must provide freedom and encouragement for participants to try new things and add new skills to their job expectations. Utilizing their new skills has to be reinforced by leaders. This is how learning sticks. This is also how CEOs ensure that the time, money, and effort they put into leader development are not squandered. In addition to allowing for learning application and modeling, leaders must also emphasize the importance of learning by tying it to the business strategy.

> *Utilizing their new skills has to be reinforced by leaders. This is how learning sticks. This is also how CEOs ensure that the time, money, and effort they put into leader development are not squandered.*

Oliver Group works with President and CEO Mike Shaver of Children's Home & Aid, who required all of his direct reports—and their direct reports and their direct reports—to participate in our programs. Even though the development was widespread, after its completion, Shaver perceived his direct reports weren't leveraging what they learned. Being an engaged CEO, he stepped back to observe what was happening. He noticed teams were working in silos and arguing with one another. He identified that team dynamics were barriers to applying their new development.

With Shaver's guidance, this organization was able to turn things around. During an interview with Shaver on my podcast— *Who Will Lead? Your Company. Your Future. Are You Sure Your Leaders*

Are Ready?—Shaver shared with me some of the actions he took to reinforce leadership with a previous company he led:

> One action was my own recognition of the value of leadership. This meant I had to change out some C-suite leaders. This gave me no pleasure, but after ten months in my role, it was clear to me that we weren't aligned about our strategic future, and we weren't aligned about the urgency to do the work. I had to course-correct the trajectory of the organization.
>
> Once we were through that change, and I reconstituted the executive leadership team, I began to emphasize the importance of a completely aligned executive team as my top priority. Nothing else was more important. This meant shared priorities, complete transparency, and absolute clarity about what we would achieve in the short term and our aspirations for the long term as well. It also meant aligning the teams that each of these executives led around leadership priorities.
>
> We supported this work by developing leadership competencies across the organization and were clear about what that looked like for an executive team, for a senior management team, and for regional leaders across the state.

One of the reasons Shaver saw success was because he made leadership a top priority, created transparencies around leader expectations, and helped direct reports apply their learning immediately in ways that applied to their specific role within the organization. In short, he created a culture that valued working together and utilizing new skills.

As Shaver exemplified, it is a CEO's responsibility to drive leadership learning. Cohorts can go through various programs, but if the development isn't leveraged, the CEO needs to identify why. Only when senior leaders get involved and reinforce the application of development with leaders will the team experience the same measurable outcomes that Shaver did.

For more interviews with CEOs and senior leaders, visit my podcast at www.JenniferMackin.com.

---

4. Learning Must Be Supported through Feedback

One powerful way to reinforce learned behavior is through peer interaction extended beyond the program itself. Each participant of programs can choose a peer from the same cohort to work with after the program ends. I see strong leaders succeed because they meet regularly and talk about their progress. Since both cohorts learned the same content, and both are trying to make it work, it can be invaluable to have somebody at their own level with whom to share.

Feedback from peers, bosses, or others is critical because participants don't know how the change they are making affects others. Encouraging and supporting feedback allows them to gain a new perspective on how their learning fits into the greater organization.

When discussing the importance of feedback in *The Succession Pipeline*, authors Drotter and Prescott claim the reason most senior leaders don't measure progress and provide feedback is because they don't realize it's their job or they don't know how to do it. Reinforcement, however, is not a secret formula. It's done by each leader creating a cycle of application and reinforcement, with everyone involved. I call this the Learning Loop.

THE LEARNING LOOP

After many practice/feedback loops,
we ultimately have to measure behavior change.

Ideally, when cohorts return from programs, they need to practice what they learned, receive feedback from their supervisor, and start the cycle over again. They can get feedback from peers, a boss, a mentor, a coach—in fact, the more the better at this practice point.

As an example of this feedback loop, a client leader returned from a program thinking she had communicated her strategy and how her direct reports fit into it. When she received feedback from her direct reports, however, she realized they didn't know the strategic foci and that she hadn't communicated clearly or often enough. This feedback gave her the opportunity to remedy this communication lapse and ensure that all direct reports understood the strategic goals.

BENEFITS OF LEADERS PUTTING LEARNED SKILLS INTO PLAY

In addition to learning and development benefits, there are other paybacks for leaders, teams, and organizations when leaders implement new skills. CEO Mike Shaver shared with me that after he acted to reinforce his direct reports' learning, he saw several measurable outcomes:

> After taking steps to reinforce learning, I saw progress on three fronts. First, we clarified where we wanted to have impact. Second, we strengthened our financial position by making business decisions and exiting programs not aligned with our desired impact. Third, we saw growth in programming that was aligned with our desired impact.

> None of that would have been possible without having clarity in leaders and in the organization about where we were going and how we would get there. I saw direct and tangible results after intentional leadership work and now recognize it's a necessary prerequisite before you can achieve anything. Even when you feel the pressure of time to do a quick turnaround, and you're really trying to see movement on the bottom line, it really has to start with leadership.

If leaders across the organization are practicing their learning and believing that their role is to develop others, then there's collaboration across all areas of the business. If they have a broader strategic understanding of how this all connects with each other and within all the departments, that's when the culture of the whole company changes. That's one reason it works and "sticks."

If you're in finance, for example, in a program with a peer in IT, then you're learning about the other's department and how the company works. You both get more out of your development, because you're reinforcing the concepts with each other—practicing, developing, and partnering. This precludes silos and gives the organization the added benefit of engagement and collaboration.

Every leader struggles with the same challenges. Collaboration allows them a resource to turn to when they are struggling. When it's built into the culture, it's encouraged. In addition to the learning aspects, this creates resilient teams that can fortify any organization.

BARRIERS TO LEADERS PUTTING LEARNED SKILLS INTO PLAY

Like the other drivers of leader development success, there are common barriers to its success, no matter your organization's size, industry, or age. As we will learn, some barriers are easier to fix than others.

BARRIERS TO LEADERS PUTTING LEARNED SKILLS INTO PLAY:

- There are time concerns.
- Senior leaders don't know how to hold leaders accountable.
- There is a lack of leadership mindset.
- Leaders don't see it as their job.
- There is no reinforcement through performance reviews, feedback, compensation, etc.
- Policies and practices get in the way.

The main reason leaders don't use the skills that they learned is because of time. For the real estate investment trust company we discussed at the opening of the chapter, this was a huge barrier. Because their industry was growing rapidly, it created high pressure for leaders at all levels. They didn't feel they had the resource of time to devote to encouraging adoption of learning and measuring the success of programs.

Furthermore, though the senior team and leaders *wanted* to be involved, they didn't really know how. This is when coaching would be beneficial, but because they opted not to spend the time and money on coaching, they didn't bridge this gap in their knowledge, so the barrier remained.

Learning is essentially about building muscle memory. This is why understanding the role of coaching is so important. Regardless of whether inside or outside coaching is used, leaders must begin to repeat newly learned skills so that the new learning becomes integrated instead of having to reference their materials for how to implement new approaches or concepts.

When I was new to leadership, I remember always having the noble intention of coaching—of asking a lot of questions and letting my direct reports find their own answers. Inevitably, however, I'd find myself telling them what I thought they should do because it seemed so clear to me, and sharing my thoughts was an ingrained aspect of my leadership mindset. Instead, I should have allowed direct reports to come to their own conclusions, and they likely would have been better conclusions than mine. A true leadership and a coaching mindset must become a habit so that all leaders at all levels develop muscle memory and help one another. Practicing it in the real world is the only

> *A true leadership and a coaching mindset must become a habit so that all leaders at all levels develop muscle memory and help one another. Practicing it in the real world is the only way the learning is going to become habit.*

way the learning is going to become habit.

Another reason leaders don't implement the skills they learned is because they don't actually see developing others as their job. It doesn't feel relevant to them, so they don't take an interest in it. Even if they see the value of developing people, they aren't measured by people readiness—through performance reviews, feedback, compensation—so there is no real accountability. This is one of the reasons that senior leaders must get involved in people development. It's not a box to check off and be done with. It requires larger, organizational reinforcement, and sometimes that's the greatest barrier of all.

Organizational policies and procedures can also be inherent barriers. When leaders aren't involved or don't see development as their job, then there is no hope for connectivity between policies and procedures, such as conducting performance reviews, compensating people, or hiring new employees. These types of systemic matters also allow for behavior change. As organizational development researchers noted in the *Harvard Business Review*, if top leaders aren't willing to change their systems, they're setting their leaders up for failure:[89]

> HR managers and others find it difficult or impossible to confront senior leaders and their teams with an uncomfortable truth: A failure to execute on strategy and change organizational behavior is rooted not in individuals' deficiencies but, rather, in the policies and practices created by top management. *Those* are the things to fix before training can succeed longer-term. It's much easier for HR to point to employees' competencies as the problem and to training as the clear solution. That's a message senior

89 Michael Beer, Magnus Finnström, and Derek Schrader, "Why Leadership Training Fails—And What to Do About It," *Harvard Business Review*, October 2016, https://hbr.org/2016/10/why-leadership-training-fails-and-what-to-do-about-it.

leaders are receptive to hearing.

Senior leaders and HR managers, leaders deserve better! You cannot point fingers at employees for failing to put into play the skills they have learned. It is a failure of senior leaders when their policies and practices aren't created to support and encourage behavioral change.

In order to allow your leaders to develop their full potential and utilize new skills—skills that your organization has spent time and money building—it is up to senior leaders and HR managers to look closely and ruthlessly at how learning is reinforced. In order to bolster your leaders, teams, and organizations, you must remove the barriers standing in the way of your leaders and their development.

MIKE SHAVER, CEO OF CHILDREN'S HOME & AID, ON LEADERSHIP:

I had to do three things [to reinforce people development]. First, I had to make it meaningful by acknowledging what development we had done and reiterate that it was a priority.

Second, I had to make it manageable by understanding the scope of the development. That meant we weren't going to use one training program for everyone; rather, we were going to be strategic about the parts of the organization that we tackled. That helped people understand this was a process—a manageable process. I was also transparent about our successes across the entire organization. When we announced promotions and elevated some of the graduates of those programs, we made clear that this kind of movement in the organization was possible because these people had participated in our leadership development program. Furthermore, it was important that these stories come from the top of the organization, not just within a division. I also communicated these to my board because I wanted them to understand that the return on investment for this kind of leadership development was actually showing results and we were getting the right people in the right positions in the organization.

Third, I made it clear that leadership development was not extra, not optional. If you can't be clear that this is embedded in the daily operations of the organization, then it's hard to sell people on the idea that it's critical to success. It's crucial that leaders be clear that leadership development is a driver for getting results across the entire organization.

For me, people development is essential for success. The most important thing a leadership team can do is to support people at an organization and to make sure they agree that development is an absolute priority. It's vital that the entire leadership team understand that our first priority as an organization is to constantly ask ourselves, *How are we investing in talent in the organization?* Nothing gets greater returns on the rank, file, and talent across the organization than effective leaders.

I reinforce this message by keeping eyes on the work that my team is doing in leadership development at all times. I let my direct reports, HR leaders, and the entire management team know that the development of our people—and especially leadership development—is our commitment.

Staff development also extends to making sure that our managers, supervisors, and leaders across the organization understand their best and highest use as leaders within our organization.

CHAPTER 8

Face Time over FaceTime

S everal years ago, I worked with a large financial organization headquartered in Chicago. Despite their limited learning and development resources, they were enthusiastic about the program we developed and the outcomes we offered. They wanted all leaders to get the content they needed, by level of leader, within a short period of time so they would be equipped for the next stage of their business: extreme competition. They were on board with the content and the leadership culture shift, but then the head of HR asked: "How can you put this online?" I explained that it's not an online program because we don't believe digital learning offers the same outcomes as face-to-face learning for this type of leadership development. She responded, "Well, that's the platform we need." She explained they didn't have enough resources for development, and the senior team agreed that they couldn't spend a lot of money on learning. They also didn't want to pull their people out of the field.

Ultimately, they decided on a plan: they would pay many outside vendors to create content for an online learning environment where a learner could customize their development. Afterward, the head of HR would be notified as each leader had completed the development. Could it be *that* easy? When I realized we were obviously not a good fit for their organization, I asked if I could contact them in a year to see how their digital learning program worked. They agreed.

A year later, I attended a large chief learning officer (CLO) conference for some of the largest organizations in the country. While I was there, I met with a senior learning and development employee of that same Chicago-based financial company. I asked how the digital learning went, and she responded, "Oh, *that*! It didn't work at all, so we threw it out the window. There's a few things still left online, but not much." I couldn't help but wonder how much time and money they spent transitioning to digital learning only to discover it fell short. I asked her why they abandoned it, and she said, "We couldn't get broad adoption, and we were only measuring completion and not skill development or behavioral change."

After our conversation, I continued to think about the future of development as I perused the conference vendors, most of whom were technology companies. Many were offering to put all learning in one place for leaders to access. It sounded so easy, but I'd heard that before. I wanted to determine how these technologies could help my clients, but as I talked more with the vendors, I didn't see anything new to advance learning.

I decided to question some senior learning leaders at the conference about their experiences using new development technologies. I asked fifty senior learning leaders of the top companies represented at the conference the same question: "Would you prefer to have your leadership development online?" All answered yes, and many said it was because their leaders were asking for it. I followed up with, "Can you point to an example of where you've seen online leadership development work—meaning cohorts became better leaders after their online work?" Not one senior leader could. I realized these leader developers were trying to implement technical changes without knowing the outcomes because that is what many senior leaders were asking for. They were basing programs off hope, not results.

> *These leader developers were trying to implement technical changes without knowing the outcomes because that is what many senior leaders were asking for. They were basing programs off hope, not results.*

As leader developers, we need to continually look at how technology can create the best environment for learning. At this point in time, despite the convenience and ease of digital learning, we don't have proof that it works. (I can almost hear the collective groan from learning officers!) This doesn't mean we don't keep attempting to leverage technology for ease and cost savings, but let's use what's proven.

Like any people developer, I strive to get clients what they want, but in the case of digital learning, they might *want* it, but truthfully the technology isn't there yet. Simply put, it doesn't enable the same experience as face-to-face learning. In fact, there is minimal research on digital learning in the corporate environment. There are people who offer online content, but there is little evidence of outcomes that deem it successful. That speaks volumes about the problem and points to the need for the Fourth Driver of Leader Development Success: *Leadership development must have face-to-face components.*

THE PROBLEMS WITH DIGITAL LEARNING

Whereas the first three drivers of leader development success are based on historical problems, digital learning presents us with a new problem. Since traditional leadership development has always been face-to-face, digital learning is a new territory to consider. We all agree that technology affords us many conveniences. Where it falls short, however, is in the learning sphere. In fact, it goes against all we have *proven* to be true of adult learning.

Face-to-face learning has historically been the only mode for learning, but it also serves as a proven model. According to *Harvard Business Review* research, studies have shown "learning happens best when learners collaborate and help one another. Knowledge—both "know-what" and "know-how"—is social in nature. It is distributed within and among groups of people who are using it to solve problems together."[90] It is difficult to replicate the social and collaborative nature of effective learning in a digital module.

In order for learning to transpire, cohorts need to apply their own experiences, challenges, and successes. Founder of eLearning Industry's Network Christopher Pappas asserts that past experiences play a pivotal role in adult learning. Since adults have decades of academic and social learning behind them, Pappas claims facilitators have to "feed into what they already know. Piggy-back off that and launch new concepts."[91] If cohorts bring their experiences to the programs, they will be able to help others learn and put new information into what they already know to be true.

---

90 Mihnea Moldoveanu and Das Narayandas, "The Future of Leadership Development," *Harvard Business Review*, March-April 2019, https://hbr.org/2019/03/educating-the-next-generation-of-leaders.

91 Christopher Pappas, "7 Top Facts About The Adult Learning Theory," *eLearning Industry*, January 20, 2014. https://elearningindustry.com/6-top-facts-about-adult-learning-theory-every-educator-should-know.

Traditional face-to-face learning works because facilitators can identify concepts, encourage cohorts to bring their own perspective to the discussion, and then learn through collaboration with one another. If, for example, I am teaching cohorts about the line of sight, I first need to set up the concept. Then I can ask, "Do you know what the strategic goals are of your organization?" Maybe half say they do. We ask them to list them and share a couple of examples with their table mates. Then I follow up: "For those who know the goals, how many of your team members understand them?" Since the group is face-to-face, they can discuss with each member to discern others' understanding. Then I might ask, "Do you feel connected to those goals?" Then we can talk about what line of sight is, its importance, and how to ensure everyone is connected to the strategy of the organization.

These subtleties of understanding are important to know in order for everyone to fully understand and explore a concept. As you can imagine, this example is lost digitally. When cohorts aren't together, they can't learn together. As we know from decades of research, it's the subtleties of concepts that spark interaction and collaboration, and within those discussions, learning occurs.

Furthermore, it's best when people come together face-to-face as peers to learn because it creates follow-up accountability within the group. They learn and work together to constantly improve their skills. Group accountability is a way to be vulnerable with peers. The same level of leader needs to be together to learn what they require at their level. They may not know each other; in fact, they may be in completely different departments. Nevertheless, everybody has similar problems because they're in the same organization, so you can hold each other accountable.

You can then leverage these connections to further learning

through continued interaction. You can pair people up and ask that they have regular weekly or biweekly meetings to assess how they're doing to execute their new skills and what their challenges are. This collaboration and accountability ensure that cohorts are continually developing as they go and executing their development plan.

In addition to heightened accountability, this is also a validating experience for cohorts. Leadership can feel lonely. As a leader, whom can you talk to? You can't talk to your direct reports. You might not always want to talk to your supervisor. Having someone at your own level gives you support but also affords you another perspective. You can share what worked or didn't work in your own practice and build off each other's experiences. This style of collaboration ensures that each leader has the support and the validation they need from a peer to perform at the highest level.

If we have no evidence that digital learning for leadership development works, then why are we still chasing it? Why do hundreds of CLOs from some of the largest organizations in the country come together in search of digital learning that works? Digital learning lures CLOs because of its flexibility, global nature, and affordability—but does it work? Nothing says it does. Part of the challenge is that some quality institutions like the Wharton School, Cornell, and others offer online leadership development. If they are doing it, it must work, right? Still, the answer is—no.

TECHNOLOGY'S ROLE IN LEARNING DEVELOPMENT

Whether it should be or not, digital learning is becoming ubiquitous in the business world, and it certainly has *some* advantages. Though it is not effective for all aspects of leadership development, let's explore ways digital learning can be used successfully.

WHEN TO USE DIGITAL LEARNING	WHEN TO USE FACE-TO-FACE LEARNING
• Harassment training • Company policy understanding • Onboarding policies and expectations • Culture—mission, vision, values basics • Follow-ups and reminders • Assessments • Snippet videos to make a point for learning • Prework and follow-up for leadership development • Skill-building training, like writing a résumé, filling out a performance review form, or reading a financial statement • Granular needs, like technology/systems training • Regulatory changes and/or understanding	• Skills focused on change or culture building • Overarching leadership skills • When relationships are important for advancement • Interpersonal and collaboration competencies • Case-focused learning

As we can see, there is a place for digital learning in leadership development, but it's more for granular items or supplemental development programs. In order to be successful, digital learning should not be used at the expense of face-to-face or virtual learning. Rather, it should be used to augment it.

A NOTE ON FACE-TO-FACE LEARNING
DURING A GLOBAL PANDEMIC:

As I put the final touches on this book, the medical, economic, and social sectors are being rocked by the spreading coronavirus. Overnight, many people all over the world are engaging in social distancing. Suddenly, being face-to-face is a liability, and we have to find new ways to connect with our teams, clients, friends, and loved ones. In this odd new reality, we are isolated except through phone calls and online communication. We don't have the luxury of getting together and learning from each other.

Suddenly leaders' priorities have shifted from concerns over development and metrics to safety and survival. During this unprecedented time, we have no choice but to learn through virtual means. Tools like Zoom and GoTo-Meeting are scrambling to meet the needs of not only the workforce but also the general population. There is a difference between digital and virtual facilitation. Digital is the recording and reviewing of content. Virtual, if done well, is conducting development in real time, using these video conferencing platforms, with groups coming together for learning. This type of development will be less effective, as we've outlined in this chapter, but it is still better than no development. A crisis like this requires technology to evolve quickly to offer a development model that is interactive and fosters collaboration. While we experiment with new delivery mechanisms, let's continue to measure their effectiveness and adjust as we learn more. We have turned all of our development into the most interactive virtual delivery we can with the technology we have. It will continue to improve and likely will do so quickly.

Once the pandemic is over, we will return to the more effective methods of development, as we will, no doubt, have a renewed appreciation for the learning that occurs when people are together—sharing their fears, worries, joys, and experiences. My hope is that senior leaders will learn from this sudden disruption to prioritize developing their teams to be more robust and resilient for whatever crises lie ahead.

BARRIERS TO FACE-TO-FACE DEVELOPMENT

There are many valid reasons why leader developers are looking to technology to fill the gaps. The reality, however, is that there is no evidence that these technologies enhance learning. In fact, digital learning goes against all we understand about adult learners—namely, as we learned last chapter, that adults learn best when their emotional brain circuits are activated. This is hard enough to establish human-to-human, so imagine the difficulties when learning is done computer-to-human.

So why have organizations begun to rely heavily on this impersonal method of development? Some of the most common barriers to face-to-face development are

- money,

- geography,

- requests of leaders, and

- limitations of learning development technologies.

Money is a major motivating factor for everyone, and orga-nizations are no different. People development is expensive. The Chicago-based financial company I spoke of at the opening of the chapter had more than twenty thousand employees across twenty states and more than twenty international locations. Needless to say, it would be costly to develop their people. They would have to free up their leaders, cover their travel and lodging, plus pay for facilita-tors and delivery. I understand their *hope* that digital might spare their resources, but as with many things in life, you often get what you pay for.

Geography is one reason leader development is costly, but it's also a barrier because most organizations can't free up their leaders—spread across various locations—for development. This is a common excuse and is often indicative of a larger organizational issue. Typically, leaders aren't working at the appropriate level and are doing the work of their direct reports. This makes it difficult to pull them out at the same time and get them all together. When they are working at the right level, however, they are leading their teams instead of doing the day-to-day work. This frees them up to meet with other leaders in a central location.

Another barrier is that learning and development leaders are trying to meet the needs of their senior leaders. When leaders request online modules, for example, development leaders would like to fulfill that request. The reality is, however, that using digital learning does not offer the same outcomes. They will have made development more convenient for everyone, but convenience is not an outcome that bolsters leaders and organizations. It is tough for learning and development leaders to confront senior leaders about this discrep-ancy because it puts their own jobs at stake.

Finally, the technology for learning development is limited. I wish it wasn't true, but at the time this book is written, there is simply nothing available that can equal face-to-face learning and development. Until there are advancements that can make digital learning more interactive and collaborative, it will continue to be an inferior method of delivery.

Technology isn't bad; it serves us in many ways. When it comes to learning and development, however, I want senior leaders and HR managers to question the outcomes before they transfer all their development online. The reality is, we can't point to any successful outcomes of digital learning. Leader developers need to continually adapt to the needs of learners but not to the detriment of outcomes.

> *Leader developers need to continually adapt to the needs of learners but not to the detriment of outcomes.*

OUR APPROACH TO LEARNING DEVELOPMENT

As mentioned, research shows that 70 percent of adult learning needs to be experiential, 20 percent social, and 10 percent formal. With this in mind, Oliver Group and Leadership Pipeline Institute (LPI) have partnered in a consulting approach that moves away from traditional lecturing. Using this model, cohorts are together for up to four days. During that time, lecture—considered the "formal" aspect of development—only comprises one-fourth of the total time together, spread out over four days. We first set up a concept, then talk through a model. This is followed by practice and reflection.

When we ask how digital learning fits in this learning model, it's mostly formal. You might argue there are elements of social learning, but not much. Inarguably there is no experiential learning. There is certainly no role play. There is no sharing of opinions. You can't get the 70:20:10 model except through face-to-face learning.

The benefit of approaches like the one Oliver Group offers with LPI is that it is directly related to people's work and how they think about their particular job. Furthermore, with face-to-face learning, facilitators can ensure development utilizes the Four Drivers of Leader Development Success outlined in this book. Without this alignment, outcomes will suffer, as will your teams and organizations.

Digital learning isn't currently working because it doesn't teach adults how they learn best. That doesn't mean there won't be advancements in the future that remedy this. But for now, despite its convenience, digital learning is an inferior model.

Leadership and development leaders will need to continue to prove their value by only offering programs that have proven outcomes. Senior leaders must also strive to be discerning and informed. This means we need to push for more research in the digital and virtual learning realms. We need to stay abreast of any outcomes that larger companies—who have the resources to try new technologies—report. Guiding this new research would help developers continue to customize our approaches.

Until this happens, learning developers must continue to offer programs that have proven outcomes. Using all we know of adult learning, we should stay true to the applicable, collaborative, and interactive learning experiences that decades of research has proven effective. We will continue to seek out new technologies, but not at the expense of our leaders' learning outcomes because we understand that leaders deserve better.

JAMIE SWAIM, ASSISTANT VP HUMAN RESOURCES OF FARM CREDIT SERVICES (FCS), ON LEADERSHIP:

Before coming to FCMA, I had thirteen years of HR experience. I had seen a lot of leadership development programs during that time, but I had not seen the same success that I saw at FCMA. Though the material presented was similar, the activities Oliver Group used to drive new ideas and change mindsets was profoundly different. In fact, I still remember the exercise that shifted my own mindset. The facilitator asked me to draw a line down a piece of paper. On separate sticky notes, I was to list all employees who reported to me. Then I was instructed to place all of those notes on the right side of the paper. I was to imagine that all of the employees left the organization, and I was to move those I would rehire to the left. Those I wouldn't rehire stayed on the right side. With my colleagues in the room, we discussed each "unhired" individual and what we would do to coach them and make them a "rehire." Not only had I not thought about my team this way, but I also realized that FCMA gave me permission to take action based on what I thought was necessary for my team and the results the company expected from my department. My previous companies, however, would need the permission of senior management to make these changes.

After my mindset shift, I started doing things differently. I have more 1:1 meetings than ever before. I feel confident in my performance discussions, full weekly "standup" team meetings and small break-out team meetings. I am planning more and asking my leader for the resources I need. I also have different meetings with my leader, who talks through my 360 assessment results and discusses goals around the "leading others" model. Furthermore, 30 percent of my performance goals are focused on the hiring and development of my direct reports. My team also provides feedback, and together with my leader, we create goals around that feedback.

CHAPTER 9

Check Yourself: Assessing Your Current Development Plan

One of the major reasons standard leadership development isn't working is because leader developers and senior leaders are not measuring its impact. According to Harvard Business's 2018 State of Leadership Development report, only 24 percent of organizations conduct some type of impact measurement.[92] Unfortunately, the most popular measurement tool remains the satisfaction survey, which, as we discussed, does not measure "real" learning in the form of changed behavior. Looking at those numbers, it's a safe assumption that the majority of organizations are spending their resources on programs that they have no factual proof actually work.

Instead of measuring impact, the majority are offering the same

---

92 Harvard Business Publishing, "The 2018 State of Leadership Development: Meeting the Transformation Imperative," https://www.harvardbusiness.org/insight/the-state-of-leadership-development-report/.

programs using methods that have been proven inferior—or, in the case of digital learning, have no proof at all. Or we're offering quality programs without any reinforcement, thereby losing any potential outcomes we might have garnered. Either way, we're failing our leaders, even though we know there are better ways.

Maybe senior leaders and HR managers want to measure their leader development, their outcomes, their retention, their strategy alignment, and their leader readiness, but they don't know how. Though there is a lot of information on how to measure impact of programs, there aren't resources that pull all the components together and guide them through an evaluative process. To this end, I offer a tool to measure your current development plan: The Leader Development Maturity Tool.

HOW TO USE THE LEADER DEVELOPMENT MATURITY TOOL

The Leader Development Maturity Tool (LDMT) assesses the work you're doing to prepare your leaders. When you can answer "*strongly agree*" to most questions, you will likely get good results. Depending on your level of leadership, there are varying ways to use this tool.

If you are a CEO, you should know the answers to most of these questions. If you're unable to answer these questions, you might take time to sit and rethink your current people strategy and partner with your team to identify areas for improvement. This can be a powerful opportunity to make some larger organizational changes to enhance your leader development.

Use the LDMT as a conversation guide for a meeting between human resources and the leadership development team—or, better yet, include the whole leadership team.

If you are a leader of HR, you may know the answers to

all of these questions. I do encourage you, however, to be bold and request a meeting with your CEO. Use the LDMT as a conversation guide for a meeting between human resources and the leadership development team—or, better yet, include the whole leadership team. Let it support you as you realign your organization and get all leaders on board.

If you are a leader of others or an emerging leader, the LDMT can be used to measure the overall systems and processes at your organization. If you can't answer these questions, or find some of the elements aren't in place, visit your HR liaison or head of HR to learn more. Use the questions within the LDMT to get answers that allow you to gauge the importance your organization places on your future leadership path.

The tool can also be helpful when starting employment at a new company. You could ask your leader to share an overview of the strategic plan with you, or inquire about the leadership skills expected from you, or aid you in gaining a better understanding of the way the organization hires and promotes people. This knowledge can help you find your place and purpose within the organization and allow you to chart your future there.

If you are a job seeker, use the LDMT to question your potential employer. You might ask how their people strategy is connected to the business strategy. Or how leaders lead the development. Especially if you are on a path to leadership, the tool can empower you to measure how supportive an organization will be of your development. Questions you might ask that are based on the tool are: Do you encourage development plans? Who could be my mentor for that? What development is available? If you cannot get answers to these questions, you might want to look elsewhere for employment.

Depending on your position, it's good to revisit the LDMT at least annually. It can be a useful tool, for example, for HR to show ROI to the leadership team. Consult it more regularly when you develop your people plan or when you make larger changes to ensure you are in alignment with the Four Drivers of Leader Development Success.

As we've mentioned, leader developers don't know what they don't know. The LDMT is not designed to criticize CEOs and HR departments. Rather, it is designed to help you evaluate the gaps in your own understanding. It points out where you—and your overarching strategies—might need bridges. It helps you know what you don't know. It's an empowerment tool to help you identify where your strategies and programs are failing your leaders. It points to opportunities for you to make your leaders, your teams, and your organization stronger.

Another goal for the tool is to hold leader developers accountable in new ways. As we've shown in these pages, the current leadership development plans aren't working, and our leaders deserve better. We must rewire our mindsets to expect more of our people developers—CEOs, HR teams, and leaders—in order to experience the transformational changes we need in leadership development.

Unless you've had a development program in place for a long time, the LDMT is going to feel overwhelming. Don't let it. Focus on the areas that are most important to you. Start there; work through that aspect. From there, move to others as you can and as you have resources. After all, small steps are still steps in the right direction. What should you start, stop and continue doing to ensure your development builds leaders to be ready for your future?

THE LEADER DEVELOPMENT MATURITY TOOL

The LDMT is divided by the Four Drivers of Leader Development Success: strategy connectedness, leader-led development, practice and reinforcement, and face-to-face development.

For each question, choose a rating using the scoring key below. At the end of the LDMT, you will total your points and see the outcome explanations that follow.

THE LEADER DEVELOPMENT
MATURITY TOOL SCORING KEY:

1: Strongly Disagree

No or very little work has been done in this area, and we cannot point to any specific success in this area.

2: Disagree

Some work is being done but not enough to support our leader development efforts. We cannot point to specific success in this area.

3: Agree

We are strong in this area and could use further improvement. We can point to some success, but it isn't optimal and/or it isn't being measured.

4. Strongly Agree

We are strong in this area and don't require change at this time. We can point to success, and we can measure it.

The First Driver of Leader Development Success: The Overarching People Strategy Must Be Connected to the Business Strategy

STRATEGY CONNECTEDNESS	SCORE
Strongly Disagree (1), Disagree (2), Agree (3), Strongly Agree (4)	
The senior team understands it is their job to drive development.	
The HR leader and CEO collaborate.	
The HR leader and CEO interact on a monthly or more frequent basis.	
The CEO views the HR leader as a trusted adviser when making people decisions.	
The HR leader is confident when challenging the CEO to think differently.	
Leader developers have seen the strategic plan.	
Leader developers understand the strategic plan.	
Leader developers can connect the people plan strategies to the business strategies.	
Leader developers can communicate the business and people strategies to all business leaders being developed.	
The HR department has CEO sponsorship of leadership development programs.	

The CEO is involved in leadership programs in some way (i.e., video for participants, kickoff the first day, or programs).	
The CEO includes people development in their communications to employees.	
Development metrics exist.	
The top team reviews development metrics monthly or more frequently.	
Your people plan is shared broadly throughout the organization.	
All leaders understand the business plan and their piece to accomplishing the plan.	
Leaders learn about development opportunities when they first join the organization.	
A leader competency model is in place and is tied to leader development.	
Leadership knowledge, skills, and abilities are tied to leader performance reviews and linked to compensation.	
Leadership knowledge, skills, and abilities are discussed and evaluated during review times.	
Leadership compensation is tied to the success of direct reports' development and/or advancement.	

Leader job descriptions include leadership competency expectations.	
Job descriptions for leaders include expectations for people development.	
Significant budget dollars (3 percent or more of total salary) are spent each year on development.	
Total Points Possible	**96**
KEY	
Don't be discouraged. There are several areas of focus that will start you on the path to better leader development. Start at the strategic level, and choose your top two to three.	0–25
Some areas are working, and you can build from here. Make sure not to lose what you do well as you add more pieces to the strategic development puzzle.	26–50
You have a lot of the right things in place. Focusing on a few other areas will enhance your overall leadership development success.	51–75
Impressive. You are fortunate; leader development is a focus and is visibly well executed.	76 and over

The Second Driver of Leader Development Success:
Leadership Development Must Be Leader-Led

LEADER-LED DEVELOPMENT	SCORE
Strongly Disagree (1), Disagree (2), Agree (3), Strongly Agree (4)	
Leaders are working at the right level and not working on tasks their direct reports are responsible for.	
Various career advancement paths been designed.	
Various career advancement paths been communicated to all leaders.	
Onboarding includes an overview of the strategic plan.	
Onboarding includes sharing leadership expectations.	
New leaders and their boss have the same expectations after onboarding.	
Participants of development programs regularly share their development plans with their bosses.	
A development plan is created for each participant for each program.	
Engagement surveys show employees trust leaders and feel valued.	

Leaders of leaders are prepped before and after leader programs on their role in overall success in all development programs.	
Leadership competencies are coached on a weekly basis after all programs are complete.	
Onboarding includes a review of HR processes of hiring and promotion and leaders' roles in each.	
All current development is facilitated separately by leadership level.	
Total Points Possible	**52**

KEY	
This is where you might want to pull a group of leaders together for their ideas. There are several areas of focus that will start you on the path to better leader development, and you need their buy-in.	0–13
Some areas are working, and you can build from here. Make sure not to lose what you do well as you add more to the leader-led pieces of the leadership development puzzle.	114–26
You have a lot of the right things in place. Focusing on a few other areas will enhance your overall leadership development success.	27–40
Impressive. You are fortunate; leader development is a focus and is visibly well executed.	41 and over

The Third Driver of Leader Development Success: Leaders Must Be Able to Put into Play the Skills They Learn

PRACTICE/REINFORCEMENT	SCORE
Strongly Disagree (1), Disagree (2), Agree (3), Strongly Agree (4)	
Skill development is measured for each participant and the group as a whole tied to each program.	
Knowledge retention is measured for each participant and the group as a whole tied to each program.	
Behavioral change is being measured in their leadership role for each participant and the group as a whole tied to each program.	
Program success is measured on key company metrics.	
Prior to attending any development program, leaders know the learning expectations.	
Leaders understand the development program's purpose when they sign up to attend.	
Each leader has a plan for their overall development as individuals.	
Each leader's overall development plan is shared with their boss.	
Each leader is accountable to put new program skills in play.	

Leaders connect the content of development program(s) to their career progression.	
Leader's successes are tied to their compensation.	
Leaders of the participants of development programs get involved, prior to programs, to reinforce the importance of the program(s).	
Each leader has a person to consult with about challenges, such as a peer, boss, mentor or coach.	
Total Points Possible	**52**
KEY	
Don't be discouraged. There are several areas of focus that will start you on the path to better leader development. Start with the low-hanging fruit or at the strategy level.	0–13
Some areas are working, and you can build from here. Make sure not to lose what you do well as you add more pieces to the leadership development puzzle.	14–26
You have a lot of the right things in place. Focusing on a few other areas will enhance your program success.	27–40
Impressive. You are fortunate; you work for an organization where leadership development is a focus and is well executed.	41 and over

The Fourth Driver of Leader Development Success: Leadership Development Must Have Face-to-Face Components

FACE-TO-FACE DEVELOPMENT	SCORE
Strongly Disagree (1), Disagree (2), Agree (3), Strongly Agree (4)	
Leaders are drawn to be a part of leadership development programs.	
Your development programs encourage peer interaction.	
Leaders are asking to attend development programs.	
Leaders are comfortable sharing their experience with other leaders.	
Leaders have ways to learn how other leaders are handling similar day-to-day leadership situations.	
Leaders have numerous interactions with other leaders of their level during their learning and/or to reinforce their learning.	
Each leader has a peer to check in with for accountability.	
Your programs are interactive.	
Leader development programs allow for participants to come to their own conclusions/understanding.	
Participants learn from each other.	

Participants practice their newly developing skills 70 percent or more of the total time of their program(s).	
Facilitators keep energy going in all aspects of the development program.	
Total Points Possible	**52**
KEY	
Don't be discouraged. There are several areas of focus that will start you on the path to better leader development. Start at the strategy level.	0-13
Some areas are working, and you can build from here. Make sure not to lose what you do well as you add more pieces to the leadership development puzzle.	14-26
You have a lot of the right things in place. Focusing on a few other areas will enhance your program success.	27-40
Impressive. You are fortunate; you work for an organization where leadership development is a focus and is well executed.	41 and over

YOUR SCORES FOR THE FOUR DRIVERS OF LEADER DEVELOPMENT SUCCESS:

1. The overarching people strategy must be connected to the business strategy.
Your Score: _____

2. Leadership development must be leader-led.
Your Score: _____

3. Leaders must be able to put into play the skills they learn.
Your Score: _____

4. Leadership development must have face-to-face components.
Your Score: _____

Total Points Available: 252

Your Total Score: _____

KEY	
You may be a young company or are just starting to allocate resources to development. You have to start somewhere and possibly walk before you crawl. There are several areas of focus that will start you on the path to better leader development. Choose three to five areas to start on and focus on the strategic level first.	0–65
Some areas are working, and you can build from here. You may be spending money on development without a return if you aren't focusing on all four areas. Make sure not to lose what you do well as you add more pieces to the leadership development puzzle.	66–130

You have a lot of the right things in place. Focusing on a few other areas will enhance your program success. Be sure to communicate what you are doing well to the senior team, your HR team, and all leaders.	131–195
Impressive. You are fortunate; you work for an organization where leadership development is a focus and is well executed. Think about how you can maintain this score.	196 and over

*For more information on how to improve any areas where you scored low, please visit **www.JenniferMackin.com** for ways to improve in each area of the Four Drivers of Leader Development Success.*

Now that you have done a full assessment of your leadership development, you have a better understanding of the gaps in your own knowledge, as well as the gaps in your organization's overarching strategies. Use this new understanding to gain more information about ways to bolster your people strategy and redesign it (or build it) so that it is aligned with the Four Drivers of Leader Development Success. The more aligned you are with these principles, the better results you will see in your leaders, your teams, and your organization.

CONCLUSION

Companies are the lifeblood of communities. Jobs attract people to communities, which then fuel taxes and keep others—like attorneys, banks, doctors—in business and funding the economy. Despite the economic importance of companies, without leaders, they fail. Research shows that we don't have enough leaders ready to take over the leadership vacancies that will occur as the baby boomers retire in the coming years, which puts us on the cusp of a leadership crisis.

The impending generational shifts in the workforce mean we will need to ready our leaders today for the changes to come tomorrow. Our current leaders in place are ill-equipped for their current role, let alone their future roles. Will we be ready? If we continue to use methods that don't work, then despite the time and money we devote to development, we will not have leaders prepared for the future.

We cannot simply assume the current leadership development is working. In fact, evidence points to the contrary. Without better development, companies won't grow or thrive. There is no doubt that the pace of business is driving change. If we do not have adept leaders to steady their organizations during the impending disruptions, companies will fail. In turn, our communities and economy at large will suffer the consequences.

Sound daunting? It is. When I consult with companies about their overarching development, they get overwhelmed. It's such an integral piece of success that it almost paralyzes senior leaders and HR managers. Stasis might be the easy option, but it's certainly not the viable one. For this reason, senior leaders and HR managers need a starting point followed by small action steps. They need to understand how all the pieces fit together. They need to know *why* people development is important and *how* to make sure their cultures and structures support that. The good news is that, regardless of your leadership position—CEO, HR manager, or general leader—you can take steps today to better your leaders tomorrow.

If you're a CEO, it's time to get in the game. Ask your team and HR managers as many questions as you need. Ask leaders about their experiences regarding development. Think about how you reward your leaders for leadership. If you need outside help, ask for it. You have a lot at stake, and the time to act is now.

> *If you're a CEO, it's time to get in the game.*

If you're an HR manager, connect with the leadership team. Create a plan around a few areas of opportunity. Conduct a Leader Development Maturity Tool, and assess your plan. Figure out what you think would create the most value, and then ask for it.

If you're a general leader, you should have higher expectations of your organizations and how they help you develop. Think about what you want and need from an organization. Ask for what you think will make a difference. Drive your own development. Leaders need to take charge of their own career development and be more assertive to get what they need and want. Sometimes, you're the only one who knows what you need.

No matter the position you hold, you must be empowered to enact change. This means connecting with others and finding answers to questions you have. This also means making sure that you are involved in organizations that include the Four Drivers of Leader Development Success. Take small steps in the direction of people and strategy alignment. Hold leaders accountable to drive change. Create an atmosphere that is conducive to putting learning into practice. Don't rely on methods that have not been proven effective. Instead, make sure that your development is supported by the decades of research on adult learning.

> *No matter the position you hold, you must be empowered to enact change. This means connecting with others and finding answers to questions you have.*

Senior leaders, leadership teams, and HR have to work together to discern what their people need. They must all get involved in the people plan. This alignment would allow them to get rid of extraneous development that merely "checks the box" and leaves leaders unprepared. It would allow them to shed the programs that don't lead them to the outcomes they are seeking.

Team alignment allows you to take your organization where you want to go faster. Rather than taking five years, you could have your people ready in three. With team alignment, you're more efficient. You don't waste time, people, or money. This provides huge financial gains and allows you to weather fluctuating industries and markets with ease. Furthermore, this alignment has immediate and dramatic effects on employee engagement. When the senior team is involved, HR feels regarded, leaders feel valued, and then all teams feel validated in pursuit of something larger.

There's always more work in this area, and there probably always will be. There will always be new leaders who have specific needs and skills. Senior leaders have many responsibilities, but the reality is, developing your people needs to be top priority. Make the time you do spend on development count. If you don't, your organization will suffer.

The more time you spend with leaders, the more engaged they are, which also increases their ability to absorb information. As we've explored from research about adult learning, employees are more engaged when they have input and when they see the connectivity to the strategy. Leaders will be more supportive and independent, allowing senior leaders to devote time to their own leadership skills. When leaders are developed appropriately, there's a ripple effect for other leaders and nonleaders. They all feel connected, vital. In short, they want to be there, which has traditionally been a struggle for senior leaders.

The standard leadership development is profoundly flawed. It's a bigger issue than those in the leader development field realize; it's a bigger problem than most CEOs understand. It's a bigger problem than my clients realize.

In 1950, Malcom Knowles, the leading authority on adult education and training asserted that the "major problems of our age deal with human relations; the solutions can be found only in education. Skill in human relations is a skill that must be learned; it is learned in the home, in the school, in the church, on the job, and wherever people gather together in small groups."[93] He went on to assert that:[94]

---

93 Malcolm S. Knowles, *Informal Adult Education* (Chicago: Association Press, 1950), 9–10.

94 Ibid.

this fact makes the task of every leader of adult groups real, specific, and clear: Every adult group, of whatever nature, must become a laboratory of democracy, a place where people may have the experience of learning to live co-operatively … These groups are the foundation stones of our democracy. Their goals largely determine the goals of our society.

Knowles understood how integral the role of leader was, not just for our teams and organizations, but for the culture at large. He went on to warn us that we[95]

cannot wait for the next generation to solve [our] problems. Time is running out too fast. Our fate rests with the intelligence, skill, and good will of those who are now the citizen-rulers. The instrument by which their abilities as citizen-rulers can be improved is adult education. This is our problem. This is our challenge.

Knowles heard the alarm sounding seventy years ago! When will we respond? We have to stop and think before spending resources—time, money, people—developing and delivering leadership programs that have been researched and proven not to work. Our leaders deserve better!

When will senior leaders know you have fixed your leadership development problems? When every leader within your organization has what they need to be effective at each leadership level. They don't need outside help anymore because development is handled internally. Leaders of leaders prepare the people who report to them, and that structure is part of your culture. It's how you do things. Leaders themselves understand what's expected of them, and they have what

---

95   Ibid.

they need to meet those. In short, everyone has the opportunity to succeed. Only then will the alarm quiet.

In order for this to happen, we all have to heed the alarm, recognize that leader development is a problem, and be courageous and emboldened to fix it. Even more importantly, however, we have to acknowledge that people development is important. Development needs to be fixed because it's integral to our teams, organizations, communities, and culture at large. It's time to stop failing our leaders and start the leadership development revolution.

BOOKS THAT SHAPED OUR LEADERSHIP DEVELOPMENT WORK:

- *The Leadership Pipeline: How to Build the Leadership Powered Company*, by Ram Charan, Stephen Drotter, and Jim Noel

- *The Performance Pipeline: Getting the Right Performance at Every Level of Leadership*, by Stephen Drotter

- *The Succession Pipeline: How to Get the Talent You Need When You Need It*, by Stephen Drotter and John Prescott

BUSINESS BOOKS WITH PERSONAL IMPACT:

- *Good to Great*, by Jim Collins

- *Built to Last*, by Jim Collins

- *Getting Things Done*, by David Allen

- *The Five Dysfunctions of a Team*, by Patrick Lencioni

- *Blue Ocean Strategy*, by W. Chan Kim and Renee Mauborgne

- *Start With Why*, by Simon Sinek

- *Emotional Intelligence*, by Daniel Goleman

- *Getting Naked*, by Patrick Lencioni

- *The Tao of Coaching*, by Max Landsberg

- *What Got You Here Won't Get You There*, by Marshall Goldsmith and Mark Reiter

- *The Tipping Point*, by Malcolm Gladwell

- *Execution*, by Larry Bossidy and Ram Charan

- *The Balanced Scorecard*, by Robert S. Kaplan and David P. Norton

WHERE TO FIND JENNIFER AND HER TEAMS

JENNIFER MACKIN:

www.jennifermackin.com

Podcast: https://forbesbooksradio.com/shows/who-will-lead/

LinkedIn: https://www.linkedin.com/in/jenniferolivermackin/

JENNIFER'S EXAMPLE SPEAKING TOPICS:

"Leaders Deserve Better: A Leadership Development Revolution"

"Drive Your Career: How to Grow in Your Career and Add the Most Value for the Organization"

"How to Use the Leadership Development Maturity Tool to Assess Your Leadership Development Practices"

"People Victories = Business Victories"

LEADERSHIP PIPELINE INSTITUTE:

www.lp-institute.com

LinkedIn: https://www.linkedin.com/company/leadership-pipeline-institute/

THE OLIVER GROUP:

www.olivergroup.com

LinkedIn: https://www.linkedin.com/company/the-oliver-group_2

Facebook: https://www.facebook.com/TheOliverGroup/